NO BOUNDARIES

WITHIN GOD'S WILL

Loren Cunningham
With Jeff Rogers

YWAM PUBLISHING
Seattle, Washington

YWAM Publishing is the publishing ministry of Youth With A Mission (YWAM), an international missionary organization of Christians from many denominations dedicated to presenting Jesus Christ to this generation. To this end, YWAM has focused its efforts in three main areas: (1) training and equipping believers for their part in fulfilling the Great Commission (Matthew 28:19), (2) personal evangelism, and (3) mercy ministry (medical and relief work).

Some names and identifying details have been changed to protect the privacy of individuals.

For a free catalog of books and materials, call (425) 771-1153 or (800) 922-2143. Visit us online at www.ywampublishing.com.

No Boundaries Within God's Will
Copyright © 2023 by Loren Cunningham

Published by YWAM Publishing
a ministry of Youth With A Mission
P.O. Box 55787, Seattle, WA 98155-0787

Library of Congress Cataloging-in-Publication Data — Pending

ISBN 978-1-64836-128-9

First printing 2023

ACKNOWLEDGMENTS

From its origins, years ago, No Boundaries, was meant to tell Loren's epic stories and lessons from his mission to all nations. Though he made his final journey home to heaven, none who know him will forget the courage and trust he gave while calling us all to carry on. I am profoundly grateful for his example in fighting through lung cancer to finish this book. When Loren's powerful voice finally went, his whispered wisdom continued to inspire and enrich these pages.

Thank you to the Cunninghams: Aunt Darlene, Karen, David, Judy, Madison, Kenna, and Liam for your care and love for Uncle Loren as he finished the final chapter.

Thanks to Gerard and Anna Sierksma, Auntie Dawn Gauslin, Libby Goehner, Jeff and Tracy Vanveen, Geeta M, Debbie Rottier, and all who made the priceless writing hours possible as the time drew near.

My love, Quezia, thank you for being my fellow risk-taker on this "once-in-a-lifetime sacrifice" during the early drafts written across the ocean from you, Daniel, and Alana. Thank you, my kids, for giving steadfast love and grace throughout this project.

I am also deeply grateful to my mom and writing mentor, Janice Rogers. You gifted me and many with stories and the courage to write "so those who read it may run." You and Dad give our family deep faith, joy, and love.

Thanks to Scott Tompkins for your insightful editing and kindness beyond measure. Thank you, Warren Walsh, Tom, and Terry Bragg, and all of YWAM Publishing for your key role in the mission.

Thanks to Stephen Ward for the inspired cover design. And thank you, Joel Rogers and our Innovision Studio team in Kona for helping get the book out!

Thank you, Kip Gaines, for your biblical worldview teaching that inspired part of the Feeling God's Emotions chapter. And thank you, Joseph Ouedraogo and Timothée, for helping confirm facts for the Mossi stories.

Soli Deo gloria!

—Jeff Rogers

CONTENTS

Introduction. 7

Country 238 9

Unique and Universal Callings 15

Go Means a Change of Location 21

Ride of a Lifetime 31

A Mission Without Borders 33

Five Steps to Living God's Purposes 39

A Presidential Bible Study 69

Called to the Mossis 75

Praying Without Boundaries 79

North African Interrogation 87

Beyond Nature and Nurture. 95

Laid Low in Tunisia 99

Libya, My Final Border 105

Through Libya's Front Door 111

Jesus Is Winning 121

Trillion-to-One Destiny 129

My Final Chapter 133

INTRODUCTION

You are destined for more than a remix of the world's expectations. Early in life, I knew a flesh-driven life had nothing to offer me. No purpose. No joy. No gain. There was no appeal in the weary grind of living out other people's plans.

Like most young people, I couldn't picture exactly where my life was going. I had more questions than answers. What is your purpose for me, God? How should I live my life? What should I do?

God had a much bigger plan for my life than I could have imagined, and the same is true for you. As I obeyed Him, the Lord led me a step at a time on a journey that took me to all the continents of the world. I preached, taught, sang, prayed, and handed out clothing and medicine. I did whatever I could find to do to help others.

By traveling the world and observing different cultures, I discovered my youthful desires weren't unique. Every generation in every culture is born with an intuition that says they're alive for a reason. Somehow, they know their life has a purpose. Youthful hope thrives even in the face of great difficulties.

Today's generation is wired to search. Diligent searchers scroll and swipe for possessions, love, friends, or jobs. What are the results? Only a few attain their ideal job, marriage, or status. Just when they make it, the joy of achievement can vanish. Fired, divorced, or rejected, they halt their search and join the disillusioned.

Others forego the search and settle for diversion. They click at pop-up possibilities of addiction, entertainment, lust, greed, vanity, or gossip. Can anything or anyone cancel the call echoing in the recesses of their hearts? The futility they sense blurs vision to blindness.

Still, there is a remnant in this generation. I've heard them pray like they are dying. With souls bleeding out, they cry and beg for something more. God hears their desperate prayers for justice, hope, and meaning.

"The people who walk in darkness will see a great light; Those who live in a dark land, The light will shine on them."[1]

These seekers are God's delight. There's no limit to the effects of prayers and actions guided by God's Spirit. Nothing on earth can control or contain lives fully dedicated to God. They can breach any border. Any opposition can be defeated when the remnant rises.

In these pages, I tell some of the most vivid experiences from my mission travels. I faced many difficult situations and met many interesting people who helped me discover God's purposes for my life. I have had great peace in trusting my life, my future to the Lord. Even so, as I began to understand God's desires, there were tremendous obstacles to overcome. My family, co-workers, and I faced dangers and discouragement by learning and following God's ways.

This book describes how God guided and enabled me and how He can do the same in your life. I write this with a prayer that you will find your world-defying path to follow God. My story can become a prologue for your incredible journey. Your way will be uniquely challenging, but your Guide is the same. With holy courage and trust, start your path today.

Loren Cunningham

---

1. Isaiah 9:2

COUNTRY 238

My jet soared past the Mediterranean island of Malta and over the warm blue sea as I thought about my destination—the radical Islamic state of Libya.

My diplomatic appeals and personal letters to its dictator, Muammar Gaddafi, had been rejected. I had tried once before to get into the country but to no avail. I suffered a severe injury on that trip and faced other painful trials in the desert.

Why was I pressing so hard to get into such a dangerous place? In forty years of mission service, Libya was the only country I had never set foot in. In my work with Youth With A Mission, I visited or served in 237 countries and more than 200 territories and islands. I felt a calling to fulfill this mission. In Deuteronomy 11:24, the Lord promised the people of Israel that "Every place where you set your foot will be yours. Your territory will extend from the desert to Lebanon and from the Euphrates River to the Mediterranean Sea." Israel did not complete that assignment, and I didn't want to miss my mandate to help finish the Great Commission.

Because the U.S. government considered Libya a state-sponsor of terrorism, it had broken all political ties with the North African nation. A high-ranking U.S. official warned me, saying, "I understand you live according to a higher law. We won't stop you. But if you get into trouble in Libya, we cannot help you."

I tracked our plane's southbound route on an overhead monitor. As we approached Tripoli, the Swiss Air plane's landing gear lurched into place. My watch read two o'clock as the wheels locked in for our approach.

"Here we go," I said with a nod to the two Youth With A Mission teammates I was traveling with—Magdy and Markus. A European diplomat friend helped get my visa granted during a brief easing of tension between the United Nations and Libya's violent government. But my visa was no guarantee of safety in this volatile dictatorship. If they even suspected we were missionaries, we would face jail or worse.

We expected to meet with a Libyan "travel agent." These agents were assigned to monitor each visitor and ordered to report anything the government considered suspicious. None of us looked forward to meeting our agent in person.

The few other contacts we hoped to make were with friends of friends, believers we'd never met. We couldn't meet them if the travel agent dogged our every step. If local believers became exposed for contacting foreign missionaries, it could mean their deaths.

I took a deep breath as our plane's wheels touched the ground. "Thank you, God, for bringing me here!" I prayed silently. "Guide and protect us, Lord." With Libya's secret police and no-trial executions, we needed God's help to make it home safely.

They herded us off the plane into Tripoli's nearly deserted international airport. Its marble accents and curved archways spoke of more prosperous days before Libya's oil exports had come under embargo.

Markus and I were the only non-Arabs among the two dozen passengers on our flight. The buzz of Arabic conversations hushed as the crowd approached the immigration officers standing in glass booths.

Before entering customs, I stepped into the passport check line for foreigners. I was scanning the crowd, trying to spot the travel agent, when my eyes met the amber gaze of a Libyan boy.

His curious stare seemed to say, *Who are you, really? What are you doing here?* I wished I could tell him. I wished I could introduce him to Jesus. But I stepped forward in silence, knowing I had to trust God in this dangerous situation.

Burned in Vision

Seeing the boy's face, I remembered when I was about his age, more than fifty years before. That's when my global journey began. My family was living in Los Angeles at the time, but while visiting a church in Arkansas, I had an experience that blew my young mind and shaped the course of my life.

My parents were itinerant preachers, so it was not unusual for them to speak in churches outside our region. One night, my mom preached a sermon and invited the people to pray. I came forward and knelt beside the altar's wooden rail. The next thing I knew, I saw an image so strange it was hard to believe it was happening. Though my eyes were shut, capitalized words appeared before me. They said, "GO INTO ALL THE WORLD AND PREACH THE GOSPEL."[2]

I was stunned by the bold letters chiseled into my eyesight. I opened and closed my eyes. The words were still there, mysteriously burning before me for over an hour. Even now, it is vivid in my memory.

That night, I knew God called me to go to the whole world and speak of Jesus' love. I hadn't traveled farther than a hop over the border into Mexico and Canada. Yet God said, "All the world." How do you start a journey like that? I was just an ordinary 13-year-old kid growing up in Southern California. It was impossible to understand the sacrifice and danger my call involved. I could not have guessed the joy and fulfillment ahead, either.

2.   Mark 16:15 KJV

Drugs in West Los Angeles

That night was a turning point for me. I already had witnessed upheaval and tragedy in the lives of my teenage friends in West Los Angeles. The choices we made had life-or-death implications. At ten years old, I met a new friend, Jimmy Abbot, and led him to the Lord. He was a kid with great potential, but he started using marijuana at age 12 and eventually began pushing weed. When the police came to arrest him, he tried to escape, and they shot him.

Don Bennet was another guy I brought to church. To my knowledge, he never gave his heart to the Lord. I told him about Jesus just a few days before he was murdered at age 16.

I invited another friend, Kenny Griswold, to church as well. He tried to get me to go to parties where he loved to drink. At age 15, someone murdered him at a party.

During that same time, I had other friends on the opposite side. They loved Jesus and pursued Him. So, I saw this deep contrast. I knew the stakes of following light or darkness.

Off-road Obedience

As a teenager in car-crazy California, I had a plan. I was making a good salary on my newspaper delivery job. All my earnings went into savings to buy a slick car I had picked—a blue 1939 Chevy. I had saved several months' salary to buy it when something unexpected happened at church one Sunday. Inside the sanctuary, right down in front, someone had parked a 4x4 Jeep.

My dad, Tom Cunningham, explained to his congregation about the new Jeep. "We're sponsoring a missionary out in West Africa in a village called Natitingou. The missionary is having problems getting to his churches during the rainy seasons. He needs a Jeep to get through those rough and muddy roads."

Inside, I knew God wanted me to do something. Looking over, I saw Lonnie Ketchey, the hamburger stand owner, and Herb Welch, the Sunday school superintendent, drop some money into the offering plate. There were no rich people at our church. It was a steep challenge to imagine us buying the Jeep and shipping it overseas to Africa. Nevertheless, everyone gave generously and cheerfully. I prayed and decided to give two months of my paper route money.

That little group of believers raised more money than my young heart expected. Within a few weeks, the church was able to send the red Jeep to the missionaries in Natitingou. Seeing the Jeep bought and shipped through our small church's giving captivated my imagination. Many years would pass before I would hear about that Jeep again.

UNIQUE AND UNIVERSAL CALLINGS

Giving my savings for that Jeep was an essential step for me. I'd grown up knowing the importance of generosity. I gave regularly at church. But inside, I realized the Jeep was different. I knew God wanted me to give specifically to *that* Jeep. God was teaching me to listen and obey. He was preparing me for the unique things ahead of me.

We often hear about people having a "life calling." Sometimes, people describe an individual who is a good doctor, architect, or teacher as having their profession as a life calling.

Though people may even tell you, "You've found your calling," God will call you to do many things. Following God is not a simplistic one-step process.

God does have unique callings, tailored things that are only for you. Other things are more common callings. For example, when I married Darlene, God called me to be a good husband and father. These two vital callings are not specific to me. God calls many men in the same way. No good dad would ever say to his kids, "I'm called to be a father, not a husband."

But people try to do this with God's purposes for their lives. Some seize onto the first thing God says to do and shut out everything else as a distraction from "their calling." Never assume your first step in obeying God will be your last.

It is crucial to seek a fuller understanding of God's purposes. Some of His designs are just for you—individual or even unique callings. Others are for everyone—universal callings. God calls every believer to pray, give, and communicate His truth. These are universal callings we need to pursue, even if we have a specific calling in an area such as music, preaching, education, or technology. Some wrongly pursue a unique calling to the point of abandoning all the universal callings. They say, "I can't do this because it's not my gift." However, God will give you the tools to fulfill your calling regardless of your natural abilities.

As you obey Him, God will weave your unique and universal callings into a masterful tapestry. God can take who you are, all your experiences, identity, heredity, and surroundings, and create something far beyond all that was you before. Your closeness and obedience to Him are two core elements God will forge into your destiny. Our finite minds can't grasp the unlimited potential of God's power matched with human obedience.

God will judge us by whether we obey Him or not. He will not believe any excuses we offer. One calling doesn't exclude the others.

When I met my wife, Darlene, she served God through nursing. After marriage, Dar didn't continue nursing. Instead, she began traveling and serving in missions. In time, she raised our children, Karen and David. Darlene co-founded Youth With A Mission. She has taught thousands and traveled to 152 countries. Though Dar hasn't been a full-time nurse in a long time, her skill in medical care has helped our family and many others throughout our travels. But I am grateful she didn't limit herself to only nursing!

There is no way to know all the steps before you follow God's path. Be sure you don't neglect universal callings, like giving, praying, worshiping, and communicating God's truth. Listen and obey God as you take your first step and every step that follows.

Instead of fixating on some unique calling for the future, I had to begin where I was. I gave what I had and trusted God to care for the rest.

At the time, I was obeying the call to give. I had no idea how important giving money for that Jeep would become later in life. I didn't realize that giving in God's will creates a blessing without boundaries. We never know the echoes of our call.

Though I didn't understand the significance, I kept taking steps of obedience.

Those steps led me on a perilous journey through West Africa. In the African jungles and villages, I began seeing why God had called me to "go into all the world."

Emergency Landing

We had been flying east for a few minutes out of Tambacounda, Senegal, when a dark thunderhead cloud appeared on the horizon. Misting rain gave way to large drop-lets hammering at the windshield. The jungle rainstorm rattled the fuselage and beat upon the glass. I leaned forward to try to look out.

I had just graduated from the University of Southern California in 1958, and this was my first trip to West Africa. Talmadge Butler, a missionary pilot who lived in Senegal, was flying the tiny plane. He regularly steered his single-engine Cessna without radio towers or radar for guidance. There were none in this wild part of Africa. Talmadge's wife and six-year-old son sat in the only two seats behind us. He regularly checked the compass and altimeter, keeping the plane on course.

"By my calculations, we should be halfway to our landing in Kedougou. It's a two-hour flight," Talmadge said. "But for all we know, this storm could stretch all the way to Kedougou. We'd better go back."

The plane swung around to the West. By the time we flew back to Tambacounda, the rain and thick cloud cover had hidden the grassy airstrip.

"Can you see anything?" Talmadge asked.

I shook my head. "Only rain and clouds."

Talmadge circled above the jungle area where we needed to land. I looked at the console of the plane. The red needle of the fuel gauge was tipping towards "E."

Even if we had a radio, there were no control towers to call for help. It was too remote.

"If we can't see, we can't land. Keep watching for an opening in the clouds," Talmadge said.

I kept staring downward but couldn't see an inch of ground.

Talmadge gripped the controls tightly, "We need to pray. We only have five minutes of fuel. But it's two hours to the next landing strip. We won't be able to land if the storm's full force catches us!"

His wife and child joined us in praying that God would save us. I watched as the sky grew darker each minute.

We continued to pray, and suddenly an opening formed in the clouds. At last, I could see the dark green jungle below.

"There! There it is!" I shouted.

Talmadge pushed forward on the controls and started taking us in. He pointed the plane's nose toward a gash of red dirt—a small road barely visible through the cloud break.

The wheels of the plane touched down on the muddy roadway. The mud road led us perfectly into the jungle airstrip near the Tambacounda missionaries' home. We pulled partway into an old World War II shed.

Rain pounded as I exited the plane on a low wing. Just then, the brunt of the storm arrived. I watched furious winds bend the trees downward. The gusts sent the rain on edge, soaking us as we hurried into the shed.

Discovering our arrival, the missionaries in Tambacounda drove their 4x4 to get us. Soon, we were resting at their home once again. I was grateful to be safe inside with Talmadge and his family.

In a close brush with death, perspectives change. Somehow, I could accept dying *if* it was God's will. The last thing I wanted was to die from my own foolish mistakes. *How could I only take risks God intends?* I didn't want to miss His purposes because of recklessness.

From then on, I began asking God to help me recognize things that weren't His ideas. Through trial and error and the wise counsel of others, I started discerning God's purposes. I am always learning this.

Early on, I learned that God's purposes never go against the Bible's instructions. God often confirms His intentions through godly counsel or even unexpected words from trusted believers. He can also confirm His steps through specific scriptures or surprising circumstances. And when it is critical, God will always show you His purposes personally, not just through others.

Over time, these lessons helped me follow God's path and avoid dangerous mistakes. I was learning to trust what I heard from God.

God's ways of guiding always bring us closer to Him. They build trust, refine character, and teach us about Him. I had graduated from university, but my learning continued.

Clear blue skies greeted us the following day, and we flew out on the two-hour trip to Kedougou. We landed on an airstrip Talmadge hacked out of the jungle with the help of the villagers. There in the frontiers of Africa, I would soon find honor and opportunity. It was my chance to obey my call to speak of Jesus.

Village VIP

The next day, I rode a 4x4 all the way to Banteko—a primitive village where Talmadge said no one had heard of Jesus yet.

I went to the village chief and began the traditional greeting protocol.

He shook my hand and clicked our fingers according to their customs. Talmadge translated for the village elder.

"How is your corn?" the chief asked.

I said, "I am from America. Our corn is good. Thank you. How is your corn?"

"Good," the chief answered. He continued asking about my goats and chickens. And then the chief said, "And how are your wives?"

Wives are a part of your status in that culture. The greater your position, the more wives you had. In Banteko, you could get a good wife for just one cow. Or you could get a not-so-good wife for two chickens and a goat.

But I was single! If I were from Banteko, my status would have been too low to speak to this chief.

After an awkward pause, I addressed the chief. "I have come a long way with a special message for your people. May I speak to them?"

The chief declared a holiday. He sent runners to bring all the workers in from the fields. Young and old gathered together to hear the important message.

I stood with the villagers beneath a tree and told them how God made the world and sent His son, Jesus.

As I explained the story to the tribe, I listened to the chief's responses. "Mmh, mm!" he would grunt when he understood and approved. If not, he grimaced and grunted lower, "Hmm."

If I heard that, I gave more explanation till I heard the elder say, "Mmh, mm!"

There I was, a single man in my twenties, speaking to the entire village.

GO MEANS A
CHANGE OF LOCATION

In Banteko, it became clear why traveling far to preach the gospel is essential. I knew that back in Los Angeles, even if I had a hundred wives, no one would call a holiday and let me preach to all our "villagers."

I was only a VIP because of the distance I'd traveled. Making the long trek to reach their tribe demonstrated the value of the message I was bringing. It even increased my own appreciation for preaching God's good news to the Banteko villagers.

The farther you travel, the more people will honor you and your message. That's a small part of why Jesus said to go.

I've heard some people insist that we should only rely on local workers because of language and cultural differences and the cost of foreign workers. It is costly and difficult to do effective foreign missions.

When Jesus told His followers to "Go therefore into all the world," He wasn't speaking figuratively. His followers soon began taking His message of redemption far beyond their hometowns, ultimately to the edges of the known world. We can go locally, but there is a unique advantage in cross-cultural evangelism. By going to Banteko, I saw how foreign travel dramatically improved the effect of mission efforts. It made me realize that Jesus meant what He said. "Go" means to change location.

In Jesus' hometown of Nazareth, He explained to the disciples, "Only in his hometown and in his own house is a prophet without honor."[3] Scripture says that "…he did not do many miracles there because of their lack of faith."[4]

How tragic that people in Nazareth missed out on healing and deliverance because of their hometown attitude toward Jesus. "He's just the carpenter's son,"[5] they scoffed. "And they were deeply offended.»[6] After he preached in Nazareth, an angry mob tried to push him off a cliff.[7]

Hometown prophets shouldn't expect to fare better than Jesus. If you believe God wants you not to follow Jesus' example of mobile ministry, prepare to be opposed or ignored.

Jesus tells us to go farther because He knows the alternative. He knows what it means if we stay in a hometown that dishonors locals who speak the truth. He calls us to a change of scenery that helps break down spiritual boundaries and allows people to hear the message more clearly.

Jesus' Parting Words

Sometimes, people only revere Jesus as God, holy and great. And He is. Yet, too often, people forget that He is also human. A loved one's last words are cherished. Usually, even prisoners are granted a dying request.

So what were Jesus Christ's last words before ascending into heaven? Acts 1, Mark 16, Luke 24, and Matthew 28 all describe Jesus' final instructions, His "Great Commission" that tells us to "go." Acts quotes Jesus saying to go "to the ends of the earth." Jesus says, "Go into all the world" in Mark. Luke records Jesus' commission "to all nations."

3. Mark 6:4
4. Matthew 13:58
5. Matthew 13:55 NLT
6. Matthew 13:57 NLT
7. Luke 4:29

Before my gospel singer friend Keith Green went to be with the Lord, he said, "If you don't have a definite call to stay here, you are called to go."

The end of Matthew emphasizes that Jesus' last request is not even a request. In it, Jesus says, "All authority in heaven and on earth has been given to me. Therefore, go and make disciples of all nations."[8]

To those who know who Jesus is and what He said, the Great Commission is the greatest cause known to humanity. It leads to fulfilling the greatest commandment—to love God and neighbor. To honor Jesus, we must honor His last words.

When you wholeheartedly obey the call to go, all the other questions of "where" and "how" can be answered. Jesus' final words could guide you to go across the street or across the sea. As you listen to the words of Jesus, it won't be too difficult to discover His purposes and obey.

The Most Twisted Verse

I once visited a large denomination in the Pacific that had never sent one missionary beyond their own territory. When I heard about it, I began to ask and discover why a Christian group of that size was not obeying the call to go.

One of the local church leaders said, "Well, the Bible does say to go first to Jerusalem, then Judea and Samaria, and then the ends of the earth. We're not going to the ends of the earth till we've reached our 'Jerusalem.'"

But does the Bible ever say we must reach Jerusalem first? In Acts 1:8, Jesus said, "…you will be my witnesses in Jerusalem, and in all Judea and Samaria, and to the ends of the earth." Many believe he said, "First in Jerusalem." But there is no "first" in the verse. They unconsciously put words into Jesus' mouth.

---

8.   Matthew 28:18-19a

By adding a word that wasn't there, they concluded that Jesus meant you should not "Go" anywhere until you've first reached your hometown or home country. But this is not what Jesus said or intended. It contradicts Jesus' point that they would be witnesses in all those places.

Suppose you add the word "first" and force this verse into a rigid model for ministry. In that case, Jerusalem is still not your hometown—unless you're living in Israel. Jerusalem wasn't even the disciples' hometown. This verse is giving a literal instruction from Jesus, not figurative.

Scripture does say, "repentance for forgiveness of sins would be proclaimed in His name to all the nations, beginning from Jerusalem." Jesus died and rose again in Jerusalem, and indeed, that is where the gospel was launched. Jesus told his disciples to stay there "until you have been clothed with power from on high."[9] This city, Jerusalem, was the epicenter for God's redemptive plan. But in this scripture, Jerusalem is only a city. It is not a metaphor for all hometowns. Jerusalem wasn't a symbolic reference here or even part of a parable.

We cannot let assumptions skew our understanding of God's purposes for our lives. Your mission in life should be based on what God says, not what people wish He said.

Jesus began, "…you will be my witnesses in Jerusalem…"

At this point, the disciples would have heard Jerusalem and thought, "Right! That's where He said to meet."

"…and Judea…" the Master continued.

"Yes, heading home toward Galilee!" they probably assumed.

Then Jesus says, "And Samaria, and to the ends of the earth."

"What? He skipped Galilee!" the disciples likely thought. Galilee would have been the next geographical stopping point.

---

9.   Luke 24:49 NLT

Remember what Acts says about the disciples, "Are they not all Galileans?"[10] Yet Jesus didn't even mention their hometown or region.

Many people feel like God loves their hometown or homeland more than others. The disciples were no different. They pestered Jesus and asked, "Lord, are you at this time going to restore the kingdom to Israel?"

But Jesus loves people at "the ends of the earth" just as much as people in our hometowns. He was trying to give the disciples His global vision. So, Jesus nixed the hometown mentality by skipping Galilee. He told them the actual route they would leave their homeland.

Still, the believers didn't leave Jerusalem until after violent persecution began in Acts Chapter 8. Only God knows if leaving Jerusalem sooner would have spared them from persecution. In any case, the murder of Stephen and the arrests of believers forced them to obey Jesus and mobilize. Then they went just as Jesus said—to Judea, Samaria, and onward.

Church history tells that Thomas traveled to India. Matthew went to Ethiopia. Mark went to Alexandria. Simon traveled as far as Africa and Britain.

As they traveled, new people received the gospel and became followers. A church grows when it goes. That was how it began. It is still the way the Spirit moves us today.

Moved by the Spirit

Jesus talks about miraculous power, saying, "These signs will follow those who believe."[11] For anything to follow you, you must be in motion. Jesus told us to get in motion, saying, "Go into all the world and preach the gospel to every creature."[12]

---

10. Acts 2:7
11. Mark 16:17 NKJV
12. Mark 16:15 NKJV

Many of us aren't seeing supernatural signs because we're not moving. No one can follow a parked car. The signs of the Holy Spirit don't follow "parked Christians."

Who is to go? We are all witnesses. We are all the church. People misunderstand because they think of the church as a building. It is not! It's a group of people who worship and follow Jesus. This should be obvious because no public church buildings existed until 250 years after Christ.

The church is us. The Greek word for church is "ecclesia," or called out ones. The church is a group of people "called out" by Jesus Christ.

Some parts of a church are local, while others are mobile. Don't accept the claim of some leaders that local churches are the only way God wants to spread the word. In Acts 13, Paul led a mobile church team that grew to 12 people. They submitted directly to the Holy Spirit, yet local churches recognized them as part of the church. Whether God calls you to "Go" from home to a local fellowship in Namibia or to "Go" across Asia in a "mobile church" team, it is essential to value and support both local and mobile parts of the body of Christ.

Find Your Team

A mobile church needs structure just as much as the local church. We need leaders with vision and wisdom in both local and mobile churches. Good leaders form teams that value their team members' spiritual gifts and roles. To fulfill God's purposes for your life, you will need to find your team.

I love the African proverb, "If you want to go fast, go alone. If you want to go far, go together." I believe teams are essential for completing the Great Commission. It could be wrong to send people out alone and in danger of discouragement or spiritual attacks.

Some thought Billy Graham was a loner in his ministry. But when I visited him in his home, in board meetings, and backstage at speaking events, I observed the strong team he formed around himself. They ministered to one another and helped each other in their unique roles. This team was one of the secrets of his extraordinary success.

The very identities of people on Paul's traveling team showed a God without boundaries. His team included Jews, Africans, Europeans, and people from Asia. It included both men and women. Its members could speak Greek, Hebrew, Aramaic, Latin, and possibly other languages.

Paul's mobile church touched a vast swath of Europe and Asia. Acts says, "This went on for two years so that all the Jews and Greeks who lived in the province of Asia heard the word of the Lord."[13]

This team gave a living example of a God without national, ethnic, or gender boundaries. No one could point with pride and ignorance and say, "We won't have Gentiles speak to our church!" They weren't only Gentiles.

They could not say, "Our culture doesn't permit women to speak." There was the Apostle Paul, recommending Phoebe as a deacon of the church[14] , and Junia, an apostle.[15] Paul's team didn't break down racial or gender barriers with protests, petitions, or sit-ins. Instead, they broke down boundaries by being who they were and serving God in unity as a team. They are stellar examples for modern churches all over the world.

Today's most significant mission work growth is among missionaries from developing nations. Men and women from Africa, South America, and Asia are answering this universal call to

---

13. Acts 19:10
14. Romans 16:1 NLT - See more on this in *Why Not Women?* by Loren Cunningham & David J Hamilton
15. Romans 16:7

"Go." These missionaries are igniting church growth across the globe. Their obedience should encourage the traditional "missions sending" nations to continue their mission. Every country, wealthy or poor, reached or unreached, needs the courage to send missionaries and the humility to receive them.

Even though I had grown up in church listening to many sermons on missions, I had not realized that missions are for everyone. It was hard to break from this cultural assumption. I had to grow up and go on missions myself. Around the world, I found faithful men and women serving God in Africa, South America, and Asia. They opened my eyes to see. Jesus' call to "Go" is for every believer. It is a core part of God's purpose for our lives.

Who, Me?

Traveling to all the nations seems out there for many. Just telling a neighbor about Jesus intimidates lots of people. But God doesn't start you with a pass-or-fail test to see if you can walk on water.

Jesus starts by saying, "Follow me." He gives you the first step and even extra grace to take it. Like a child learning to walk, your faith will grow through obeying each step and listening for the next.

If you fall, your Father picks you up. He doesn't reject you for mistakes. When you repent, He helps you back up, holds your hands, and guides you to take another step. Jesus didn't just put up with the people around him when He came to earth. He knew it was a "faithless and perverse generation."[16]

Yet He called them to faith and action. He invited ordinary fishermen and a tax collector to follow Him. And He is inviting us too.

16. Luke 9:41 NKJV

Jesus wanted to explain His message through Peter, James, and John. Now, He wants to use us. The disciples did it. Twelve guys from a tiny town in a backwater place unleashed a force that toppled evil empires.

As you can read in Acts, it was grueling. There were real messes to clean up. There were disagreements, organizational challenges, and even a body or two to bury![17] But they received the Holy Spirit. They lived lives that glorified God. They moved in His power.

During those days in Africa, I had yet to find my team. There were so many fuzzy uncertainties. Where should I go next? How can I help others see that this is for them, too?

In a few weeks, I left Banteko and went on across West Africa. As a young man preaching in a foreign land, I witnessed the result of going to distant places with God's message. Soon, God showed me the profound effect of obeying the universal call to give. He showed it to me with a Jeep and a little bug.

---

17. Acts 5

RIDE OF A LIFETIME

While I continued to preach in the villages of Togo, I received an invitation to cross over to Benin[18] to preach there. I jumped at the opportunity because I remembered Natitingou, the village where my church had sent the red Jeep. The coarse dirt road passed through dozens of dusty villages as we approached Natitingou.

All my soreness from the bumpy roads was forgotten when I got there and saw a red Jeep. It was the one our church gave! After greeting the missionary and his family, I asked, "Could we go for a ride in your Jeep?"

"Why, sure, Loren," he replied. "Hop in."

Like a kid, I jumped in the seat and grinned with excitement. I gave the others a "thumbs up" when the Jeep's weary engine finally cranked to life. It rocked and shuddered as it rolled down the dirt road. After all those years of use, it was about ready for "Jeep heaven."

I smiled as I exited the Jeep, wiping the sweat from my face. The hot, dusty ride was a lifetime thrill for this former newspaper boy.

That moment became a core memory in understanding that "…where your treasure is, there your heart will be also."[19] I had put an offering for a Jeep before my own desire for a car, and now my heart delighted in a bumpy ride in that very old Jeep.

---

18. known as Dahomey until 1975
19. Luke 12:34 NASB

The Red Bug Oracle

In the village, I ate and talked with the people of Natitingou. Later, they told of a missionary named Bill who had driven that red jeep to another far-off village. Bill stopped the Jeep outside the village and asked if he could speak with their chief. Curious little children gathered around to stare at the white man. A few young men took Bill to the headman so he could address their tribal leader according to local custom.

Upon meeting him, Bill said, "Chief, I want to tell you and your village about God."

"Wait," the elder answered him and turned away.

To the missionary's surprise, the village leader walked away a short distance and bent down to the ground. He searched in the scrubby grass until he found a dark red beetle. The old chief lifted the bug and placed it onto the hood of the red Jeep. The color matched.

The wise old chief then strode back to the missionary and said, "I heard a voice that said a man would come in a car this color and tell me an important thing. Now tell us about your God."

God used a simple act of a church's generosity to cross over geographic and cultural divides. God used my child-like obedience to help give a beetle-matching Jeep to the villages of West Africa. Of all people, I had the privilege to watch the ripple effect of God's blessing through that Jeep. That gift our West L.A. church sacrificed to send had no boundaries.

As you obey God in the universal callings to give, pray, and go, you cannot imagine how far God's blessing will travel. Your "yes" echoes beyond measure.

When God sees your willingness and obedience, He can reveal the dreams held in His heart for you.

While driving out of Benin on that long, rutted road, I wondered if I would ever see the people of Natitingou again. It was just a small village, but one God would use to bless the nation.

A MISSION WITHOUT BORDERS

After several trips around the world, the visions God gave me began to unfold. My efforts grew into a movement of missionaries called Youth With A Mission (many friends call it "Y-WAM").

This new mission began with short-term teams of young people. Luke 10 describes a time Jesus sent out 72 disciples on a short-term outreach. Paul and Barnabus also took Mark, a youth, on their mission journey. God gave us the role of renewing this New Testament model of youth-inclusive, short-term missions.

Our practice of listening to God and doing what He said united and mobilized believers of many denominations. By releasing men and women, young and old, lay workers and clergy, YWAM multiplied and diversified rapidly.

During the first years of Youth With A Mission, there were times when I did not see what would come next. At that point, it would have been impossible for me to understand everything God was planning. He knew there were too many obstacles and options for anyone to take on the world alone. So, He sent me the perfect help mate.

In 1963, I married my beautiful wife, Darlene, and we immediately flew to Europe for a mission outreach. Soon, we moved to Switzerland with our seven-month-old daughter, Karen. Our son, David, was born there in Switzerland. We traveled together often, sharing the thrills and challenges of serving God as the ministry expanded.

We took short-term teams of youth to every continent, including Antarctica and the islands of the world. Soon, this movement of young missionaries overflowed into different ages and nationalities.[20]

We could never have imagined the boundary-breaking ways God would use our young mission to spread the gospel worldwide. For example, in YWAM's "King's Kids" ministry, children traveled with their parents into "closed nations." They spoke of God's love to communists in Eastern Europe and Asia. Everywhere they went, God guided our young men and women to cross artificial boundaries between ages, cultures, and church denominations.

"Short-term missionaries" who joined YWAM through the Discipleship Training School (DTS) kept switching and becoming long-term staff. And retirees began to "refire" as YWAM missionaries. By 1998, there were 12,500 full-time workers, most from non-western nations.

Darlene and I encouraged these "YWAMers" to listen to God and use every tool available to share the message of Jesus. Soon, there were Youth With A Mission athletes, cowboys, filmmakers, counselors, dancers, journalists, teachers, musicians, entrepreneurs, scientists, lawyers, and others who took God's truth into every area of society.

In 1978, I met with Dr. Howard V. Malmstadt, a famous scientist and educator. He joined Darlene and me in Kona, where we pioneered a missions training campus, pre-school, and high school. Our campus became the launch point of the University of the Nations, the first truly global university with modular education. Since then, many thousands of students, representing over 100 countries, have studied in our schools.

God also used YWAMers to launch relief and development ministries like YWAM Ships, Gleanings for the Hungry, Mercy

20. *Is That Really You, God?* - tells many stories of how God started YWAM.

Works, and refugee centers in Asia, North Africa, and the Middle East.

New expressions of our three-fold mission of evangelism, training, and mercy ministries emerge daily. Over the past 60+ years, I have watched the Lord do amazing things in YWAM, but His vision for us will go far beyond my lifetime. While I cannot see the future as He does, I see a simplicity in His ways that hasn't changed in all the years I have walked with Him. He wants us to pursue an intimate relationship with Him—to call upon Him often and to listen for His voice. To respond in faith and obedience.

In this process, God began teaching me how to cooperate with His creativity. Step by step, He deepened our relationship as I listened closely and responded in faith.

Unboxing His Voice

When God put that vision in front of my eyes to "Go therefore into all the world…" God was giving me, a 13-year-old boy, one thought about my future. He was communicating just one part of His dreams for me.

It may never happen exactly like that for anyone else. Some will hear God like Elijah did, as a "gentle whisper."[21] Others will hear God through dreams, like Joseph. It is fascinating to see God's creativity in how He speaks, often in different ways with each person. I have read more than 20 ways that God speaks in the Bible. If He knows you are listening wholeheartedly, God will use uniquely personal ways to give you His thoughts.

Psalm 139 says, "How precious are your thoughts about me, O God. They cannot be numbered! I can't even count them; they outnumber the grains of sand!"[22]

---

21. 1 Kings 19:12
22. Psalms 139:16-17 NLT

With God's thoughts outnumbering sand particles, He will undoubtedly have dreams for you. He is the great Creator, and when creating something new, He often starts by building up our excitement and anticipation. If we are listening, God shares His creative ideas.

Genesis Chapter 1 gives a glimpse of the Father, Son, and Holy Spirit talking about a creative idea. Verse 26 says, "Then God said, "Let us make man in our image, in our likeness."

The thought was too thrilling to contain. God spoke it out in advance. You can see God's joy as He created new things because He even pauses to admire the work and says, "It is good."

God did not wrap up His creative endeavors on earth when he finished creating the world. God still creates in and through the lives of people worldwide. He creates new hearts, new opportunities, and, yes, "new creatures in Christ" (2 Cor 5:17). Scripture also says Jesus is creating a place for us to live in Heaven.

In the book of Isaiah, God says, "Forget the former things; do not dwell on the past. See, I am doing a new thing! Now it springs up; do you not perceive it?" (Is. 43:19)

The earth was commanded into existence by the creative power of God. An intricately designed universe could only come from a Designer like Him.

If atheist apologist Richard Dawkins is correct, then the universe has "no design, no purpose, no evil and no good, nothing but blind, pitiless indifference."

You have more faith than I do if you believe that everything and everyone came essentially from nothing and no one.

So, why go on? If there is no one above nor anything to expect in eternity, life loses all reason, meaning, and love.

It is tragic to miss the reality of our loving personal Creator. God's creative personality anchors our understanding of life and destiny.

Over and over, the prophets of the Old Testament warn that idolatry makes people become like their carved idols—blind, deaf, and senseless.

It is the same today. Your outlook on life is dictated by what you serve. Many serve masters of ego, image, selfishness, or lust. Their confused and lonely lives show what those gods are like.

But the true God is near.[23] He is here, creating new things.

The Maker's Groundbreakers

As believers, we seek to live godly lives by God's grace. He is compassionate, and we are to be compassionate. God speaks the truth. So we should, too. He forgives, so we must forgive.

We know that God is the ultimate Creator, but we rarely acknowledge that He wants us to be creative—to begin new things by His grace. Though God could accomplish all His goals without human help, He chooses to involve us in His creative endeavors. The Lord invited Adam to name the animals. He summoned Abraham to become the father of a great nation. He called 12 ordinary Galileans to begin the global Church.

God loves to share the creative planning process because He loves us. He wants to spend time with us doing significant things.

Jesus says, "No longer do I call you slaves, for the slave does not know what his master is doing; but I have called you friends."[24]

God heard Joshua's prayer to hold the sun still while Israel routed its enemies. This prayer wasn't even true to physics! Joshua had no way of knowing the sun doesn't move around the globe. But our gracious God answered His incorrect prayer. Of all the ways God could've worked to save His people, he chose to listen to this inaccurate prayer.

---

23. Phil. 4:5
24. John 16:15 NASB

On that extra-long day, God demonstrated both His power and His humility. He desires to work through us, even if we don't know what to ask.

"For the eyes of the LORD range throughout the entire earth, to strengthen those whose heart is true to him."[25]

God seeks out people like Joshua, David, Nehemiah, and Ruth. He is seeking committed hearts to work in and through.

The gospel is not broken. The world's desperate problems are not from some lack of God's ability or character. He is willing and able to heal every nation's wounds. The only thing lacking is our willingness. He is ready to do it through you. Are you ready?

25. 2 Chronicles 16:9 NRSV

FIVE STEPS TO LIVING GOD'S PURPOSES

Youth With A Mission's growth over the last few decades is not the result of some slick mission strategy. Our expansion happened as we applied the principles God taught us. It now seems almost unbelievable how God has used our ragtag group to buy castles for mission campuses, to launch a fleet of hospital ships, to mobilize a quarter of a million short-term missionaries annually, and to bring education, health care, food, and friendship to some of the darkest and most dangerous places on earth. But it was real. The mission has continued to multiply.

Over these high-growth decades, I noticed five steps God led us in each time He did something new. These five apply to you too, as you seek to apply God's principles and purposes. They are simple but profound. They involve listening to God, praying His prayers, speaking His Word, feeling His emotions, and doing His works. As you follow faithfully, He will release new understanding and creative power to accomplish His intentions for your life.

STEP 1: LISTENING TO GOD

The first step in living God's purposes is to listen to God. In my first book, *Is That Really You, God?,* I explain how listening to God is a spark to ignite your life. All our global ministries in YWAM began with us seeking to hear from God. Of course, some believers think God no longer speaks or that we humans cannot hear His voice. But the whole Bible disproves this. Even young Samuel, at age five, had the experience of hearing the voice of God. All prominent, godly people in the Bible listened to God: Noah, Abraham, Moses, David, John, Paul…. A complete list would take pages.

How can an infinitely wise God ever speak to finite people? God's knowledge is great. Psalm 139 says it is beyond our understanding. Even if we memorized the entire Bible, it would still only be a tiny fraction of God's infinite knowledge. We cannot digest all His knowledge. So the Holy Spirit takes part of God's vast understanding and communicates it to our hearts in what scholars call the *rhema* word of God.

Jesus told his followers, "I have many more things to say to you, but you cannot bear them at the present time. But when He, the Spirit of truth, comes, He will guide you into all the truth."[26]

These rhema words are never to replace or add to the Bible, which is the *logos* (written) word of God. Instead, they serve as reminders or instructions for applying Biblical truth.

For example, no one needs to ask God, "Should I ever tell anyone about Jesus?" That question is answered already in scripture.

However, it could be great to ask, "Lord, now, should I tell this coworker about Jesus?" Hearing God's response to a specific question like that helps apply the truth of the Bible.

Jesus said, "If you love Me, you will keep My commandments. I will ask the Father, and He will give you another Helper, that He may be with you forever; that is the Spirit of truth."[27]

To start recognizing God's counsel, wait patiently and listen. As a boy standing by that altar rail, I committed my heart to listening to God. I wasn't aware of any steps I needed to take to hear God. I simply waited and listened.

26. John 16:12-13 NASB
27. John 14:15-17 NASB

Preparing your Heart to Listen

I have learned from teachers like Joy Dawson,[28] Duncan Campbell, and my mother, Jewell Cunningham, the importance of listening to God in prayer through the Bible. Another step of preparation is to focus on Him through praise and worship. That is how I began that night at church. I was singing the truth of who God is and what He means to me. Sincere worship helps focus our attention entirely on God. Immediately, we can begin listening for God to speak.

Sometimes, when we listen, God will reveal things in our hearts that shouldn't be there—unforgiveness, wrong attitudes, or any other kind of sin. When we repent of any sin or, if appropriate, make restitution, we open our hearts to hear God. Then it's time to ask Him to take away any distractions, whether in our thoughts or distractions from the enemy.[29]

Then, we wait silently with an expectation that God wants to speak. While praying, committing to obey what God says is essential. If you promise God you will follow whatever He says, He will find a way to speak to you.

As your relationship with Him deepens, you can better recognize His voice. It is not so much about experience as it is about a depth of trust and desire to know Him.

One time, when my daughter Karen was still a little girl, the keys to the car went missing. My wife said, "Karen, you've got to help me find my keys. Let's pray."

They prayed and listened to God till Karen looked up. "Mommy, they're under the newspaper!"

Dar reached over, lifted the newspaper, and there were the keys.

---

28. See Joy Dawson's book "Intercession, Thrilling and Fulfilling" for more on intercession / listening prayer.
29. James 4:7

With a smile, Karen said, "It's sure a good thing you have me, isn't it?"

You see? Even little children can show the elders a thing or two because of their innocence and uncomplicated trust. God has no difficulty speaking. We are the ones with a listening problem. When your heart is ready, His words come at the exact right moment.

God cares about everyday things, like finding car keys when we are in a hurry. It brings such joy when you hear God in those day-to-day settings. There are times, though, when the same simple act of listening to God can be a matter of life and death.

A Suicidal Secret

While in Tauranga, New Zealand, a few years ago, I was invited to a luncheon where Dr. Narelle Dawson, a psychologist from Hamilton, was to speak. I was seated at a table in front.

Dr. Dawson arrived a little late. She didn't even sit down but greeted us and began to tell a story about a flight she took in the late 1980's. The work-related trip meant her taking a long flight from New Zealand to Los Angeles to Dallas.

With a friendly smile, she said, "An American sat beside me in the aisle seat. He asked my name and where I was from. I answered politely but thought, *He is probably one of those Christians.*"

"I remember thinking, *Why did I have to end up next to someone like this?* I had been an atheist all my adult life. At my office in New Zealand, I only hired atheists. I didn't believe in God and didn't like being around people who did."

"I thought, *If I could just get this guy in for some counseling sessions, I could cure his delusions*," she recounted. "But then the man turned to me and said something that shook me deeply. He said, 'I believe you have a problem with suicide.'"

Dr. Dawson looked down, "There was no way he could have known. I had never told anyone, but I had attempted suicide five times.

"Too shocked to react, I sat while the man took a piece of paper and wrote out two lists with scriptures next to them. He explained to me, 'These are the steps that lead to suicide. This other list shows how to be free from those causes,'" Dr. Dawson continued.

"By then, we were getting ready to land in Dallas. He gave me a book that I packed away. I didn't read it till I was back at my office in New Zealand. In front of my workers, I read the whole book through to the end."

Smiling again, she continued, "After I finished the book, I knelt down, and accepted Jesus. And every day since then, I've started my day with Jesus."

"You know, that piece of paper… I have moved four times in the fifteen years since that experience. And I always carry this paper with me," she unfolded the paper and held it up.

As soon as Dr. Dawson lifted the paper, I recognized it. It was my writing!

And she pulled out the book and said, "This is the book that American gave me."

It was an old copy of *Is That Really You, God?* Dr. Dawson opened it and showed us where I'd signed it.

"Oh, my! I had forgotten!" I exclaimed to Dr. Dawson. I stared in wonder at the book and the crinkled paper she held.

A YWAM friend of hers who knew her testimony had arranged her talk to surprise me. What a wonder! Hearing God's voice on a long-forgotten plane flight saved her life and her soul.

God invites us to join Him, whether He is saving lives and souls or finding the car keys. He says, "Ask me, and I will tell you remarkable secrets you do not know about things to come."[30]

It starts by understanding His thoughts and then praying in faith to see them happen. He asks us to inquire, "God, what do you think?"

---

30. Jeremiah 33:3 NLT

Listening to God naturally flows into the next part of living God's purposes: prayer.

STEP 2: PRAYING GOD'S PRAYERS

Seeds get scorched. Many who begin pursuing God's desires get shut down immediately. It happens if you take the first step to listen but fail to move on to prayer, the next step. God's purposes can be mixed up, postponed, or even destroyed without prayer.

Prayer is our continuing conversation with God. It involves asking questions, presenting our needs, expressing our concerns, and waiting for the Lord's responses. Sadly, many never experience that type of relationship. They think prayer is a sentimental wishing, expressed to a heavenly Santa Claus. But that's not it at all. No amount of wishing something was true, thinking or saying positive things, or pledges of good deeds will have the effect of a sincere, humble prayer. We cannot manipulate God, and to try to do so cheapens our relationship with Him. By asking for things with a selfish motive, we hinder the close relationship God desires to have with us. Or, by asking without believing, we treat God like He's not our real heavenly Father.

God is not a deadbeat dad who abandoned you. He was never a heavenly great-grandfather, blind and deaf to your prayers. God is not divorced from your life, trying to bribe you for affection and presents. He's a better Father than our hearts can fathom.

Instead of approaching prayer like that, realize that prayer is participation. God has all the power, yet He responds to our requests. He delegates authority to the people He made.

God spoke out an idea. He said, "Let us make human beings in our image...They will reign over the fish in the sea, the birds in the sky, the livestock, all the wild animals on the earth."[31] So God did it. He made men and women and told us, "Be fruitful and multiply; fill the earth and subdue it; have dominion over the fish of the sea, over the birds of the air, and over every living thing that moves on the earth."[32]

When God gave people dominion over the earth, it meant responsibility for what happens here. God will always be on the throne. Any authority we have is delegated from Him. So, we should be all the more careful about how we exercise this dominion.

He entrusted a perfect world to humanity. But from the beginning, people squandered our dominion over the earth. Worse, people's actions and attitudes rejected God and gave away authority to the enemy. From the Garden of Eden till today, people gave dominion to darkness.

God cut the puppet strings. He gave us perfect freedom to know His love and pray, 'Your will be done.' Prayer is exercising our spiritual authority. It is using dominion for the exact reason God gave it.

Jesus taught us to pray, "Your kingdom come, Your will be done." Through prayer, we use our authority on earth to invite God to do what He already desires. You listen to Him and learn His will, then pray for that with faith. You can participate by asking and believing His words. Your prayers change the outcome as you ask for God's will to be accomplished "on earth as it is in heaven."

"What is man that you are mindful of him?"[33] the Psalmist asks. It is a good question. Can't God act without us? Of course. He is sovereign. He is a King who can do whatever He desires. But throughout the Bible, we see God reacting to prayers from

---

31. Genesis 1:26 NLT
32. Genesis 1:28 NKJV
33. Psalm 8:48 NKJV

Abraham, Moses, Solomon, Samuel, Daniel, Hezekiah, Nehemiah, Hannah, the disciples, Paul, and others.

Don't take God's authority on prayer lightly. Prayer means participating in God's divine actions. There is no experience like it.

God is an extraordinary Father. He lets the sons and daughters He's adopted participate in His works. After listening to God and learning His divine purposes, use the dominion He has given you as His child. Exercise your authority and pray for His will to be done here and now. The more you pray in the will of God, the more God's kingdom will come "on earth as it is in heaven."

I watched this happen overnight in the life of a young communist philosopher from Beijing. My brief encounter with him revealed the vital importance of prayer in living God's purposes.

A Beijing Philosopher's Prayer

Foot traffic was nearly at a standstill at 5 p.m. as thousands of Chinese crowded a Beijing sidewalk. YWAM leaders Peter and Luba Iliyn walked along with Darlene, David, and me. Karen was teaching at the time in Hong Kong. We made our way as best we could through the crowd until a friendly young man emerged to introduce himself. He said he was a philosopher and wanted to practice English.

"Oh, come talk to our friend Loren. He's a philosophy graduate from USC," Peter invited.

The friendly Chinese man with a gray suit and tie came over. Peter said, "Loren, I'd like to introduce you to Sikong. He's a philosopher from Peking University."

I shook his hand, saying, "Good to meet you, Sikong. What is your main philosophy, then?"

"I am a dialectical materialist," Sikong answered with a hint of a British accent.

It makes sense. That's the Marxist philosophy China adopted.

"That is interesting," I said. "I've studied that. But please, tell me more about it. The question I had was, How do you have value for yourself in this kind of philosophy?"

We discussed his philosophy back and forth as the sun fell below the horizon. The crowd kept passing by like a tide of faces. I liked the young man. His reasoning was sincere. He wasn't just using slogans as a front for an intellectual ego.

Peter and Luba were waiting. They seemed to be praying silently for Sikong.

At one point, I said, "All of us sense that we have some value. Let me tell you my philosophical view."

I said, "There is a personal and infinite God, and we are made in His image. He gives us value and even loves us. Without value, we cannot have meaningful love."

For six hours, he debated with me on this. Then I asked Sikong, "But what do you do with guilt?"

The handsome Chinese scholar nodded, "Now that's the real problem. There is no one to forgive us."

I knew a door had opened, so I explained, "We do make wrong choices and carry guilt from those choices…but God can forgive us. He can forgive you."

By nine o'clock that evening, Sikong believed in God. By eleven, he had prayed and became a follower of Jesus. He wept as we prayed together in the cool night air. God's love and forgiveness filled his heart. The philosopher became a newborn believer.

I told him, "I'd like to give you a Bible because it is God's word. Can I send you one?"

"Oh, no!" Sikong shuddered. "My only address is one I share with my boss. I could go to prison if he knew what you sent me."

"Besides, I am leaving Beijing on Monday," he said.

"Really, where will you go?"

"My boss won't tell me. He will tell me on Monday before I leave. He only said it is a big city in the South."

How will he get discipled? I was momentarily worried, but I realized what to do the next instant.

"That is no problem," I told him. "We have a living God. And God's Holy Spirit will guide you to the right place and people to help you grow in your faith. Let's pray!"

Peter, Luba, and I prayed with Sikong. Then I said, "Now we're going to continue praying. And you keep praying, too. In the city you go to, you will find a group, maybe just a small group of people, that have met Jesus like you have. They will love Jesus and love each other. They'll help each other and other needy people, too. This group will also worship and pray together. If they can, they will study the Bible together. This is how you will know they are real believers like you are."

We all said goodbye to Sikong, and in the morning, we departed on the Trans-Siberia Railway to Mongolia.

Less than a year after we met Sikong in Beijing, I flew back to Asia again. In Hong Kong, I met with YWAM leaders working inside China. One of them approached me and said, "Sikong says to say 'hello' to you! I'd told him I was coming to meet you."

"How do you know him?" I asked, surprised to hear the name.

"He found our YWAM prayer group," the man explained.

I smiled and gave my co-worker a pat on the back. Wow.

In a Chinese city with millions of people, God had led Sikong to a YWAM group! We had never even told him about YWAM. We just told him to look for people who loved Jesus. God answered our prayers despite Sikong's communist boss and countless unknown obstacles.

It is a wonder to see how God led Sikong. Effective prayers aligned with His design made what seemed impossible a reality.

As you begin discovering His purposes, you activate them through prayer. From prayer, you move to the third part of living God's purposes, speaking out His words. But before you speak out, there's an internal barrier to overcome.

Avoiding the Fatal Mistake

Some people listen and pray a little and then quit right there. "Oh, I was given a vision! Isn't that wonderful? Now it is sure to take place," they think. But to receive God's dreams and not act on them is wrong.

The Lord may be calling you to a prayer initiative, but don't just toss out a token prayer and avoid the work God called you to do. Ever since God had Adam name the animals, God has sought to involve people in His work. He does not push us away and say, "Just leave it to me."

The fatalistic idea that God's work is God's problem is a concept of false religions. It has nothing to do with Jesus' words and teachings. Fatalism, or the belief in absolute fate, is to think or live in a way that says, "Everything is up to God."

It sounds pious to wait for fate. But this concept has disturbing logical conclusions. If God alone is responsible for everything that happens, He is the source of all disease, suffering, and violence.

When a true fatalist looks around and sees the fallen world, he thinks God is to blame. But God is not responsible for the agonizing results of our sin.

Jesus said, "Every tree that does not bear good fruit is cut down and thrown into the fire. So then, you will know them by their fruits."[34]

False religions aren't the only ones who harbor fatalism. Fatalists who claim to be Christians will not have good fruit

---

34. Matthew 7:19-20 NASB

either. You won't recognize fatalists by their actions but by their inaction. They have given up on reaching the world, waiting complacently for Jesus' return to whisk them from all troubles.

Of course, Jesus is coming. However, if we were supposed to accept the world "as is," then Jesus would not have said to "Pray earnestly...[35]» There would be no need to "Go therefore and preach the good news." Good works of charity, education, health care, or relief would be pointless or wrong.

No. Jesus loved us more than life itself. He gave Himself to give us life. And in turn, He commands believers to go and give that life to all creation.

So, we must refuse fatalism. We go to extremes instead, like Jesus, who laid hands to pray for lepers and chased out money changers who were defiling the temple.

God's love drove Him to action, and it still does. His passion should move us to action, too. The fact that He's returning should accelerate our efforts. He wants us to pray His purposes into existence. Faith-filled prayer will motivate us to action, not apathy. This is what it means to live God's dreams. We get the design from God and then pray and persevere till it comes into being.

In a sense, our faith is like a muscle that pulls those invisible thoughts, God's dreams, into life. He holds out something and says, "I want you to have this." And we respond by saying, "Thank you, God. Please let me have that."

The exchange may seem strange. Why not just give it? But we do the same. We teach children to ask politely for things they need. This helps build up their character.

The Bible calls faith "Now faith is the certainty of things hoped for, a proof of things not seen."[36]

---

35. Luke 10:2
36. Hebrews 11:1 NASB

God is teaching us faith and faithfulness. He knows we'll need them for what is coming. Consistent trust and obedience invite God to reveal His great designs. Without willing obedience, we would face catastrophe.

We push past generic, boring prayers by listening to God and praying His prayers in faith. We don't have to pray, "God, please help poor people worldwide."

Who knows if God heard or answered a prayer like that? The prayer is so vague that nobody would see the result even if it did happen. When we pray for a specific community or people group, we connect with God's heart. He hears and will respond to prayers spoken in faith.

Some pray, "If it be Your will…" before asking for anything from God. But if we listen to know His will, we can pray in detail. We can have the excitement of seeing specific prayers answered.

Often, we shy away from powerful, world-changing prayers because we fear shame or disappointment. We don't want to ask for the wrong thing and become disillusioned. We can avoid such discouragement by listening and praying specifically according to His will. This will change your life. You will find yourself praying for things you never imagined.

God would never set you up with unrealistic expectations. He knows precisely who you are and who you can be. "'For I know the plans I have for you,' declares the LORD, 'plans to prosper you and not to harm you, plans to give you hope and a future.'"[37]

If Israel, a judged and conquered people, could receive this promise, can't you accept it too?

The Father is holding out his dreams, offering you His hope and future. But you must exercise your faith by praying and asking.

---

37. Jeremiah 29:11

God tells Israel, "In those days when you pray, I will listen. If you look for me wholeheartedly, you will find me. I will be found by you," says the LORD.»[38]

If you understand and fully participate in God's purposes, you will be living your destiny. That's because destiny is not just a dream of the night. Destiny is not a mirage in the distance. Destiny is a man named Jesus. You were born with a purpose: to know Jesus and live like Him. This is the highest dream, calling, or destiny you can ever hope for. Any other godly desire you have or will have will guide you to Him. He is "the Way."

It is electrifying when you know you are participating in God's work and getting closer to Him. It is sometimes hard to contain the excitement.

Soon, you will be ready to speak out about what God shows you. After listening and praying, speaking out God's purposes is the next step.

STEP 3: SPEAKING GOD'S WORDS

After listening to God's thoughts and praying His prayers, at the right time, you speak it out. By declaring what you've heard from God, you take the third step to create something with Him and others. This life-transforming move might not happen if you don't speak out.

As you speak out, there can be problems and even persecutions to overcome. Speaking His words exposes assumptions, fears, misunderstandings and opponents of God's intentions. It is critical to share God's words at the right time with the right people.

In 1974, I received word that *Time* Magazine writer Richard Ostling wanted to report on Youth With A Mission as a follow-up to his landmark piece on the "Jesus Revolution" in 1969.

38. Jeremiah 29:12-14a NLT

We wrote back, pleading with them not to report about YWAM. "This would destroy everything God is trying to do through us. We're trying to get authenticity, not publicity."

The timing and audience were all wrong.

When the stakes are high, it can help to talk with a mature believer you trust. Sometimes, they can either affirm a "God idea" or help you avoid unwise ideas of what you think God wants. People's trust in your character and abilities often grows as you grow in faith and obedience. Jesus grew "in wisdom and in stature and in favor with God and all the people."[39]

As you interpret what He's put on your heart, be careful to make it clear what are your personal words and what you believe He is actually saying. Do share your heart, but be clear. Never manipulate by describing your personal opinions as God's.

Declaring God's idea sparks His design into action. But it also can have a nice secondary effect. Speaking out God's purposes will give listeners a chance to know God better and befriend you too.

Speaking out God's words was a crucial part of Jesus' work on earth. When Jesus healed or performed miracles, He would say things like: "Your faith has healed you" or "Get up and walk!"

I imagine Jesus could have just waved a wand like a magician or his hand like a "Jedi" to do whatever miracle. Instead, He spoke out words with the authority to bring freedom and healing. By speaking God's words out loud, Jesus drew multitudes together to a voice they could trust.

There are many other ways to heal, preach, or teach, but if you pay attention to Jesus' life, you see Him constantly modeling the way we are to live. As Isaiah wrote about Jesus centuries before, "'They shall call his name Immanuel' (which means, God with us)." He lived every moment as "God with us."

---

39. Luke 2:52 NLT

In seeking to pattern our actions after His, it's easy to see Jesus didn't respond to each person the same way. With some people He healed, Jesus told them not to tell anyone. With another, he said, "Go home to your family and tell them how much the Lord has done for you."

We need that love that discards catchphrases and one-size-fits-all communication. Our skeptical world can easily spot insincere messages and poseur messengers. Slick talk cannot convey something as profound as God's message. Speaking words of truth and life takes more than just memorizing scripture. To speak out God's intended messages, we must know what to say and how to say it. The previous steps of listening and praying are essential for speaking God's words.

Speaking at the Mosque

In 1988, I walked through a quiet cobblestone street tucked away in the capital of a Central Asian nation. The friends I walked with slowed down and passed through a gate into a large household. Delicately painted landscape murals adorned the walls and ceiling.

At this home, the father was an imam, the influential leader of many mosques. His wife and children smiled as I approached the imam and shook his hand. They had welcomed Darlene, David, and me, a Christian missionary, into their home as a special guest.

According to their custom, he gave David and me embroidered hats and robes to wear. Then we sat down for a beautiful feast in his home. The family laughed and chatted together. It was easy to see their love for each other. We enjoyed eating and talking together through a good part of the afternoon.

Then the imam asked, "Would you like to go with me to my mosque?"

"Yes," I replied.

So the men went together to the new mosque that was under construction. My eyes were drawn to the minaret tower, shaped almost like a queen's crown. Our small group passed beneath a curved arch and entered the mosque.

Inside, the imam introduced me to some of his leaders and said, "Would you please tell them what you believe about Jesus?"

Surprised by the imam's request, I thanked him and began speaking.

They all knew Jesus as a prophet. The Koran calls Him Issa. So, with that foundation, I began to talk about why God sent Jesus. I told them how Jesus came for our redemption.

While I spoke, one of the leaders started turning angry. I wasn't surprised. Here I was speaking about Jesus in the middle of their mosque!

"Do you believe in three Gods?" he shouted. "Why? There is only one God!" The man kept jabbing questions, and I continued answering, but I knew my words were only skimming the surface of a deeper issue.

God, what should I do now?

While the questions and answers continued, I heard God say something very unexpected in my mind.

Apologize to him for the Crusades.

It had never occurred to me that the ancient wars Christians waged on Muslims mattered to modern Muslims.

"I want to ask your forgiveness," I said to them.

"What have you done?" the man questioned.

"It is not anything I have done. But it is something that people did in the name of the one I serve," I answered. "It is something Jesus never would have wanted, the Crusades."

I later learned that local television stations would play and replay movies about the Crusaders attacking Muslims. The injustice was being relived again and again through the people's entertainment. It was no wonder his anger was so fresh.

"Only God can forgive," the man said, waving a hand to dismiss my apology.

"Oh no," I shook my head slowly. "We are to forgive too. God forgives to show us how to forgive." I continued talking about forgiveness for a minute or two.

Then, the man abruptly ran out of the building.

Uh, oh. What is he going to do now?

The moment he left, everyone's attention went to the imam. He nodded, encouraging me not to stop because of the distraction. I kept teaching and answering their questions. With the angry man gone, they could ask more personally meaningful questions.

Then, while I was mid-sentence, the man who had rushed out burst into the mosque. His breath was short from running. He slipped off his shoes and made a beeline for me. In his hands, he held a large bunch of grapes. He stopped before me and stretched out his arms to offer them to me. I understood. They were his way of expressing forgiveness to Christians for the Crusades.

I reached out and received the gift, thanking him. Inside, I also was thanking God. He'd given me wisdom for how to speak to this man.

Years later, I returned to visit the imam and discovered he was now the leader of more than a thousand mosques.

He told me, "One of my purposes in life is to ensure peace between Christians and Muslims."

Later, I received word that he gave his heart to Jesus on his deathbed.

By speaking the words God wanted, I was living His purposes. I do not know how many lives were touched by my teaching in the mosque that day. The results are always in God's hands.

Jesus said, "...do not worry about what to say or how to say it. At that time, you will be given what to say, for it will not be you speaking, but the Spirit of your Father speaking through you."

God will give you the words when you listen and obey Him.

As you start living God's purposes, you may wonder, "Will it ever really happen? Are our prayers just pretend?"

These doubts don't have to stop us when we know God has spoken. We can push through with prayers and words of faith.

After listening and praying, God will show you when to speak His words. Then, the message comes to life. You could be called to talk to friends at church, a family member, or even in foreign situations like at that mosque.

God says in Isaiah 55, "So is my word that goes out from my mouth: It will not return to me empty but will accomplish what I desire and achieve the purpose for which I sent it." That is precisely what happens when you allow God to guide your words; they don't return empty.

To bring God's kingdom to earth, we listen, pray, and then speak His words. Once the words ring out, a new phase of living God's purposes begins—feeling His emotions.

STEP 4: FEELING GOD'S EMOTIONS

Does God truly have emotion? Some suggest that scriptures like "Jesus wept" or "God was grieved in His heart" are simply examples of "anthropomorphism." It is a long theological term meaning God only does or says something to act it out for us. In other words, He's pretending something to prove a point.

These theologians propose that God is not joyful, sad, or angry. In anthropomorphism, He's supposedly just trying to help us understand things. This implies that God has no real feelings.

I believe God is not faking anything. When the book of Zephaniah says, "He will rejoice over you with singing," it means precisely that. When Genesis says God's "heart was filled with pain" over the peoples' sin, I know it is true. He experiences genuine emotion.

Since God is passionate about us, how should we be? We are to be moved by God's passion. God stokes our hearts as we listen to His words, pray His prayers, and speak the words He gives us. When you live God's purposes, He fills you with His zeal and passion. There is no way to be numb and indifferent when close to God. God isn't like that.

Feelings of hurt and hatred were inflamed during the years of apartheid (racial separation) in South Africa. During that time, Joy Dawson, Brother Andrew, and I traveled there to speak at a Christian conference. The racism and oppression we saw there were undeniable, as the country's laws unjustly favored white South Africans while segregating and dehumanizing the rest of the population.

"We don't want apartheid liberalized. We want it dismantled," declared Anglican archbishop Desmond Tutu. "You can't improve something that is intrinsically evil."

At the conference, the three of us prayed and spoke the messages God put in our hearts. The people immediately responded with prayer and action. Many white Christian leaders knelt and began washing the feet of black South African pastors. For some, it was an act of personal repentance. For others, it was a collective repentance for the sins of white South Africans.

As they bent low and removed the shoes of the black pastors, the sound of weeping began to fill the room. In their humility, they touched the heart of God. Tears fell from my eyes and those around me. We all felt God's heartbreak and grief over the nation's hatred and injustice. That day, I experienced a remarkable charge of God's emotion that I have not let go of. I wept with the crowd in a public way I have rarely done before or since.

If God says, "Let it go," then I do. I let Him visibly express joy, sorrow, and other God-given emotions. That day in South Africa was a remarkable charge of the Lord's emotion that I have not let go of to this day.

As we live His purposes, God can speak to us through emotions in a personal and profound way that can be private. Others would not realize it is happening, but when it is Him, it is clear. However, with my personal feelings, it is more complicated. Inside, I recognize a generational hindrance in expressing emotion publicly. While I feel emotions deeply, I seldom speak of them.

Expressing emotion within the church triggers concern and judgment in parts of the body of Christ. Some people reject true miracles and scriptural gifts of the Holy Spirit as "pure emotionalism." I have witnessed people whipping up emotion based on emotion alone, without any apparent response to God's Word or character. Shouting at the Lord rather than listening to Him does not resonate with me. He hears. He knows. Do we?

As pastors, my parents were well aware of this dynamic. Our response was to keep extreme emotion at home rather than in public. They sought to preach with passion, not emotionalism. But knowing the difference is difficult. Hearts, minds, and emotions are not neatly dissected when God's Word comes alive. I try to let His Word be living and active, to show me what is what.

Though I do not want to create stumbling blocks of division, healthy public expression of feelings should not be repressed. If it will help us grow or heal in a godly way, so be it. Paul writes, "For the kind of sorrow God wants us to experience leads us away from sin and results in salvation. There is no regret for that kind of sorrow. But worldly sorrow, which lacks repentance, results in spiritual death."[40]

---

40. 2 Corinthians 7:10 NLT

So, are we to be stoic and unfeeling? Or are we to work ourselves into an emotional frenzy? Neither. Feeling personal emotions is right when they don't lead us astray. And feeling God's emotions is right but not something forced.

Above all, we must not manipulate ourselves or others through emotions. Let God Himself speak through His emotions, with words or without.

The life-shaping decisions He intends are not rooted in emotional reaction. God has given you a measure of authority on earth and the ability to choose or refuse His ways.

Think of an 18-wheel truck with a big load hauled behind. The truck is like your will. It steers the direction your life will take. Emotions should be like the load carried behind. They make life vivid and should not be abandoned. But the will has to be in front, the feelings in back. Otherwise, your truck would jackknife.

Mindlessly following people or emotions won't realize God's designs. When you pursue God's purposes, His emotions can spill into your heart.

"Clap your hands, all you nations; shout to God with cries of joy," the Psalmist exclaims. Like David, we can rejoice in God's works. Like Jeremiah, we can also lament with Him.

Faith allows your heart to understand what God's doing. Then, emotion begins to overflow. So don't be surprised when it happens.

You may not be prone to shows of emotion, but if God's Spirit is moving, and He says, "Let it go," do just that. It is part of the flow of God's purposes expressed through you.

To live God's purposes, we first listen and pray, steps one and two. In the third step, we speak out. These first three steps touch you with God's feelings before you take the final big step.

STEP 5: DOING GOD'S WORKS

My wife, Darlene, often tells people we can't take credit for starting Youth With A Mission. "It was all God," she says with a smile. "The only thing we can claim is that we didn't give up."

It's true. We do God's works like toddlers help with chores. Though little children may pick up toys or even push a broom, the parents' guiding hand gets the job done. But even with the guidance of God's thoughts, prayers, feelings, and words, it is still a challenge not to give up doing His works.

The book of James reminds us, "Faith without deeds is useless."

We are not saved by doing God's works. "For by grace you have been saved through faith. And this is not your own doing; it is the gift of God, not a result of works, so that no one may boast." (Eph 2:8,9 ESV) But what did God save us for? The following verse answers by saying, "...we are God's workmanship, created in Christ Jesus to do good works, which God prepared in advance for us to do."

Grace is not just for keeping us from sin and lifting us if we fall. It allows us to take daring actions that are impossible without God.

You enter God's destiny by creating with Him. You fulfill your life's purpose by doing the steps mentioned above—listening to God, praying His prayers, speaking His words, feeling His emotions, then going all the way to the final step of doing His works. These individual parts of living God's purposes are not always sequential. They can be, but often it varies.

Sometimes, God doesn't wait for you to pray or feel before He asks you to do something.

The process of living God's purposes is not some strict formula. This is only a rough sketch of what it might look like.

Don't get lost in the steps. Just keep close to God as He guides you and reveals His love. Even though these steps are clear, their path is narrow. To do God's will means doing it His way, in His timing, with His right motivation.

Sounds difficult, right? In fact, it is humanly impossible. But God's grace is super-human. And His Spirit lives in every believer.

It is easy for us to make mistakes. We can get confused, have the wrong timing, or allow pride to abort God's purposes. This doesn't mean there is a weakness in God's design. The weakness is in us.

If we ask, God's Spirit can purify our old patterns of sin. When we stumble and make mistakes, He lifts us from the pit and sets us on a firm rock to begin again. Many of God's purposes have not been realized. He wanted to live with people in the perfect garden of Eden.

God also designed Israel to stretch all the way "from the desert to Lebanon, and from the great river, the Euphrates—all the Hittite country—to the Great Sea on the west. (Joshua 1:4)"

Was this realistic? To this day, Israel has never stretched that far. What could cause the Israelites never to get the whole promised land?

There must be something more precious God seeks—something a promised land and a garden paradise cannot deliver. He wants your heart. He cares about you more than His purposes for you.

It is foolish to shrink back in fear of messing up God's designs. God is not afraid to let go of His own garden and nation—if only our hearts would come home to Him.

His ultimate dream is not gardening in Eden or real estate in Israel. He made those designs to relate to us, work with us, and make us one with Him. When people messed up the first design, He devised another and another. What a humble Creator! He catches us when we fall. He finds us when we wander. He binds our self-inflicted wounds.

History is His story of forgiveness and redemption. Your history, whatever mistakes you've made, can also be redeemed. You can be a part of His story.

"Behold, I make all things new!" Jesus declares in the book of Revelation. With every new purpose, God's goal is the same. He wants our thoughts, prayers, words, emotions, and deeds to be made one with Him. He wants us.

That is why He sees our hearts' weaknesses and still speaks out His purposes. It's all part of His greater purpose to "Go and make disciples of all nations."

God wants your heart focused on living His dreams. He wants willing hearts to carry His message of love. God could always do everything without us, but He chose to include us in His purpose to save the world.

Inexperience or inadequacy is no excuse for avoiding God's purposes. He is willing to risk the reputation of the King of Kings to involve us in His purposes and call us His ambassadors. God will intentionally lead you to do works that are beyond your capability. He led David, a little boy, against a Philistine giant. He sends us "as sheep among wolves." God shows you a "promised land" and then helps you take it by force. Anyone walking God's narrow path will face those kinds of challenges—to build faith and trust.

He knows what you can and can't handle better than you do. Only God knows you well enough to determine what you are capable of. It was clear God knew more than I did when he called me as a boy and sent me as a young college graduate into the bush of West Africa.

In the following years, I visited every continent and continued living God's purposes. The world grew smaller while my call grew larger. Traveling from nation to nation, I saw that God didn't have dreams for me or some, but for the entire world.

God, the Mapmaker

By the time I'd been to about 100 countries in missions travels, I realized that nations have personalities just like people. I would ask God, praying, "Lord, give me an understanding of the destiny of this land. Let me participate in some way to bring them into Your destiny, Your purposes, Your callings for them."

I knew God had destinies for nations because Paul told the Athenians, "From one man, he created all the nations throughout the whole earth. He decided beforehand when they should rise and fall, and he determined their boundaries. His purpose was for the nations to seek after God and perhaps feel their way toward him and find him—though he is not far from any one of us."[41]

So God creates each of us, and He establishes each nation. He even draws the borders. The Mapmaker does all this so people will "seek after God."

Armies battle for borders. People die over borders. Nations make and break treaties about borders. Throughout history, people have formed countries by either separating or thrusting together different people groups. After World War II, generals of the Allied forces drew new "lines in the sand" to define the nations of North Africa. Their maps' bizarre geometric borders make it obvious they did not follow natural boundaries or the territories of people and language groups living within them.

Yet the Bible says God "determined their boundaries." He also decides the sequences when nations will "rise and fall."

Jesus said, "And this gospel of the kingdom will be preached in the whole world as a testimony to all nations." It's often hard to perceive God's work on the world's boundaries, but sometimes, you can glimpse it as you seek His will for a country.

41. Acts 17:26,27 NLT

In 1985, I was invited to speak to more than a thousand believers in Finland during the height of the Cold War. As I listened to God in prayer, He said, "The Soviet Union will soon open. Speak it out!" So I stood on the stage and said, "Openness is coming!"

In my heart, I felt the Lord say, "More! More!" So I said louder, "Openness is coming! Openness is coming to the Soviet Union!"

Doubtful stares and dead silence were the crowd's only responses. They looked stunned. They probably couldn't believe I had said it. A Finnish publisher friend told me later, "I thought you went over the edge, Loren."

But the following year, the communist leader, Mikhail Gorbachev, announced that a policy of "glasnost," the Russian word for openness, would begin in the Soviet Union.

In 1988, I traveled to speak to a crowd of 11,000 at the Messe Exhibition Hall in Frankfurt, West Germany. As I prayed, God gave me another shocking word.

"Get ready! Prepare, because God wants to bring down the Berlin Wall. He wants to bring into one the two nations of East and West Germany," I told the crowd of German believers. After the message, some angrily approached the platform, "How can you say such things!" one woman said.

No one had ever thought that the communists of East Germany would peacefully reunite with West Germany. It was a radical political statement, especially since it came from me, an American missionary.

I answered her, saying, "I'm just the messenger. It's God telling me what He's going to do." I knew that He is the one who sets the borders.

Soon, a man wrote an entire book denouncing people who say things like this as "false prophets" and naming me specifically. People were outraged. On January 19, 1989, Erich Honecker, the dictator of East Germany, said, "The Wall will be standing in 50 and even in 100 years." But that year, Honecker was removed and arrested. The wall was torn down, and Germany began to reunite.

After the wall came down, I did an extensive speaking tour of Germany. While there, a group of more than 300 government leaders invited me to discuss their newly reunited nation's identity and role in the world. I spoke in Berlin on the very day Soviet tanks and troops were leaving East Berlin.

I stood before a crowd of over 80,000, including Germans and visiting Christians who had come to tell Germany of Jesus' love, saying, "Today, the Soviet armies have marched out of Berlin. Today, an army of Christians has marched in!"

I spoke to them about God's purposes for them as a nation. "You began modern missions through the Moravian movement. You were the first nation to print Bibles. You did it on the Gutenberg press that Germans invented."

The words echoed through the large stadium as I recounted the story of Germany's downfall. Satan was so afraid of the church of Germany, he tried to destroy them through Hitler's lies. By 1945, there was no Germany. It was all occupied territory.

"But now is the time for the resurrection of God's call for Germany! Now Germany can become a greater force for missions than ever before in history." These experiences showed me clearly that God decides nations' borders and times. I did not doubt as I watched God fulfill His words about the Soviet empire and Germany. He understands each country's unique personality and character. He knows nations like we know people, only better.

God can speak to nations like people, giving them hope and meaning. So He is undoubtedly able to guide you. You can listen to God's guiding words for your life. And you can listen to God's guiding words for your nation. Both you and your country need to know God's purposes. God is drawing and redrawing the maps to work on the hearts of each nation. You can either seek Him and obey Him or ignore and reject His will. The decision is yours.

A PRESIDENTIAL BIBLE STUDY

In 1991, our family joined a team aboard YWAM's *Pacific Ruby* that visited the remote South Pacific island of Pitcairn, the last territory on earth to receive Youth With A Mission missionaries. I had visited more than 235 nations and dependent countries by 1996. During my missionary travels, I'd spoken to kings and heads of state in Tonga, Norway, the Netherlands, and other countries. Still, it surprised me to get a call at our home in Switzerland from a representative of the president of Benin in West Africa. I pressed the phone close to my ear. *What did the president of Benin want from me?*

"President Kerekou wants you to teach him to be a righteous leader so we may become a nation that would please God," the assistant told me. The man explained that two years ago, Mathieu Kerekou had renounced atheism and his communist dictatorship over Benin. He even apologized to the nation for leading them the wrong way. After calling for a democratic election, the people chose another man. But one term later, Benin chose to re-elect him as president. Mr. Kerekou had read my books and wanted to meet me.

Wow. After gratefully accepting the invitation, I hung up the phone. I thought of the Jeep ride in that little village of Natitingou, Benin. Half a century had passed since our church had given the red Jeep. I took a deep breath and sat on our living room's white couch. When Darlene came in, I told her about the phone call.

"Oh, Loren, that's wonderful!" Dar said with a hug.

As I packed, I asked the Lord, *What are your purposes for Benin?*

I knew it wasn't enough to speak of their hope for eternity—they also needed hope for today. Through my travels, I knew that each nation has gifts and callings. Many African countries have more believers per capita than countries in Europe or North America. But governmental corruption and poverty drown their hope of becoming nations that glorify God.

Millions of Africans have dedicated their lives to Jesus in a prayer of salvation. Each man and woman who becomes saved begins being renewed. But what about their government? What about their schools? What about their workplaces? Each nation and believer must be discipled. We can't become complacent after a new child of God is born. No loving mother finishes giving birth and says, "I'm glad I'm done with that baby!" Delivery is when the work has just begun.

It is hard enough to care for your own family; how can we care for the world? Many believers feel satisfied if the family can attend church together. The family and church are two essential domains of society. But if God's ways are rejected in government, business, science, education, media, and arts, even righteous, church-going families will suffer greatly.

I boarded a train to Zurich to catch my flight to Benin. My heart was charged and ready as I prayed. I arrived in Cotonou, Benin, and the president's guards escorted me off the plane. They took me into a large waiting room in the airport. To my surprise, the news media of Benin were all there for a press conference with me!

"Why have you come to Benin, Mr. Cunningham?" one reporter asked.

"I was told of how President Kerekou has become a believer in Jesus, and he wants me to teach him how Benin can become a nation that pleases God."

"Did you know that President Kerekou was an atheist and the dictator of Benin for seventeen years?"

I nodded to the reporter, "Yes, I did. But he apologized for leading you into communism. And He allowed a free election. He let you vote him out of power. But now your country has chosen him to lead you again. Benin has a special opportunity to turn toward God and receive His help."

After the press conference, a black Mercedes took me to the presidential palace. President Kerekou shook my hand warmly and motioned that I take a seat.

I laid my Bible across my lap and asked, "Mr. President, before I teach you from the Bible, may I tell you a story?"

He nodded, folded his hands, and began listening carefully. I told the president about "some newspaper boy" in California and the red Jeep his church sent to Benin. "At the church in California, a preacher explained how the Jeep would go to a missionary who needed it to reach his churches near the remote village of Natitingou." At that instant, the president's brows lifted. He leaned forward.

"That newspaper boy grew up and visited Natitingou as a missionary," I continued, explaining about the chief's red bug and the joy of riding in the Jeep." I know that was a thrill for the boy because that newspaper boy was me," I finished with a smile.

"Aha! Ha Ha!" the president laughed, then looked at me intently." Did you know that Natitingou was my home village? I grew up right there!"

"Natitingou?" I gasped.

"I was probably there when you came as a young man," the president said, shaking his head in surprise.

Then I opened my Bible and began sharing with the president. I showed him principles on how to rule Benin with righteousness, to help it become a nation dedicated to God. President

Kerekou was eager to learn God's Word. When I finished and prayed for him, he said, "Would you also teach my government leaders?" He took me to meet his cabinet and their deputies. There were about forty of them. Before sitting down, he whispered, "And begin with the story of the jeep."

For an hour, I spoke to these leaders of Benin. Only one of them was a believer. The others followed Islam or voodoo. Benin is the birthplace of voodoo in West Africa. I spent a long time teaching these men from the Bible and answering their questions.

"Now is the time for Benin!" I said. "There is no reason Benin or any nation must remain impoverished through corruption. There is no limit to what God wants to do through you!" After I boarded the plane to fly back to Switzerland, I looked through the airplane window. Below me was the busy patchwork of Benin's capital. As we climbed into the blue, the homes and cars grew smaller and smaller. I leaned back against my seat and thought of the great potential in this one man.

President Kerekou's desire to learn God's ways was the most extraordinary element. I remember how eagerly he followed along as I showed him what the Bible said about government.

God sees the whole picture—every life, every thought, everyone, everywhere. The Lord loves to use ordinary people of faith to confound the "wise and learned" egotists of the world. When anyone faithfully listens and obeys Him, God can position them to do the most excellent good possible.

God is the only one with the heart and the authority to always do what is best for us and our nations. It is no problem for God to place people in critical roles of authority in government, education, business, science, media, or entertainment.

What the Creator wants is a remnant, people who will pray and act in obedience. Even Sodom and Gomorrah would have been spared if ten righteous men were in it. Ten men aren't enough to win a vote or even form a successful protest. God does not need a majority vote to save our cities and nations. He only seeks devoted people with enough faith to take action.

If you live without limits on God's purposes, it is even possible to have a righteous legacy beyond your lifetime. I realized this when I learned about a spiritual renewal spreading over multiple generations in a tribal group called the Mossis.

CALLED TO THE MOSSIS

A few years ago, a YWAM worker told me about an American man in the 1920s who was praying for Africa. While he focused on God, he heard the name of a tribe in Africa—the Mossis.

Through the years, the man never visited Africa but asked missionaries who visited his church, "Have you heard of the Mossis?" The answer always came back, "No." He kept praying for the Mossis. He prayed they would hear the gospel and come to know Jesus. Eventually, God told the man to travel to Africa and find this tribe. He talked to his boss, explaining what he was going to do. "I'll see you when I see you," he said to his employer before departing in a large ship to Dakar, Senegal, the westernmost point of Africa.

Upon arriving in Dakar, the man went into the busy marketplace daily and asked the people he met, "Do you know the Mossis?" No one knew the Mossis. After six weeks, he finally met an African man who said, "Yes, I know the Mossis."

Where are they?" he asked.

"Oh, very far. The Mossis have a big, big village called Ouagadougou. It is a long way."

"How do I get there?"

The Senegalese man pointed east and answered, "You walk that way."

Overjoyed at the news, the American gathered supplies and began a trek of 1,200 miles through malaria-infested regions until he reached the sprawl of Ougadougou in what is now Burkina Faso.

"God, I have found the Mossis!" he prayed. "What should I do?"

To his surprise, he felt God answer, "Go back to America and tell everyone you know to start praying for the Mossis." Again, he obeyed. He returned to America and told everyone he could find to pray for the Mossis. After some time, seventeen families heard the call and went to minister to the Mossis.

A Royal Mossi Missionary

One of the first Mossis who became a believer was an 18-year-old man who was royalty among the tribe. Not long after his salvation, the young man became a missionary himself, rejecting the role of emperor of the Mossis, a feared tribe of horsemen. He began preaching and starting churches till he lost his wife. He moved back to Ouagadougou and married again. Just after he reached age 60, the man's second wife gave birth to a child named Paul Dangtoumda.

At age 18, Paul joined Youth With A Mission and became a missionary. From Africa, he went to study in Europe and then Hawaii. He graduated with honors from YWAM's University of the Nations. Paul went on to teach and preach extensively. After years of faithful mission service, he founded a UofN campus in Port Harcourt, Nigeria. He trained hundreds of youths for missions and for careers aimed at reforming every area of society.

I traveled to Nigeria in 1991 to speak at the University of the Nations campus. I met Paul and his wife, Rachel, and their two daughters there. By then, Paul was old enough to have flecks of gray in his hair. The Port Harcourt campus had grown to have fifteen nationalities and several schools. When I stood with Paul and the people there, I thought back to the faithful prayer of a man on the other side of the world, two and a half generations ago. His prayer in the 1920s started it all.

This prayer crossed over generational boundaries. It passed over national borders. The prayer echoes on.

The Legacy of an 80-Year-Old Prayer

Those prayers are still being answered generations later. Simon Compaoré, the son of the first preacher from that first generation of Mossi believers, became mayor of Ouagadougou and then Minister of State for Internal Security.

Timotee, another Mossi in Youth With A Mission, said, "Simon Compaoré's father was one of the first Mossi pastors. Now Simon is changing Ouagadougou." Smiling brightly, he explained, "The streets are cleaner. Prostitution is not allowed. New jobs are being created, and people are jailed for corruption. They are afraid to steal money because there is no forgiveness for this," Timotee laughed.

When talking about Compaoré's effect on the nation, Timotee said, "I cannot believe it! I cannot explain it! It is amazing how God changes a country."

Joseph, another Mossi YWAMer, agreed, "Ouagadougou was really just a big village before. In French, we say, 'une gros village.' If you went to Ouagadougou in the eighties and returned now, you would not recognize the place. Simon Compaoré did a great job. He works so hard." Joseph said, "The country is growing stronger because there are a lot of Christians getting involved in the government."

The Mossis are still blessed by the legacy of a man who obeyed God to pray and journey to a tribe he'd never known.

PRAYING WITHOUT BOUNDARIES

It is an extraordinary privilege and responsibility to pray without boundaries. As with this man's prayers for the Mossis, your prayers have no expiration dates. There are no geographical limitations either. As a child of God, you can listen to God and obey this universal call to prayer.

Without prayer, you cannot expect to see God's purposes fulfilled. It's impossible to do God's works without Him. You literally "haven't got a prayer."

Many try to do God's work without His power, but disappointing results and the exhaustion of striving grind them to a halt. If anything positive does happen, it's only from the effects of someone else's prayers. So be careful to lay a foundation in prayer for any Kingdom work you seek to launch. This applies to evangelism, pastoral counseling, teaching, and worship ministries. It also affects people who seek to glorify God through services like health care, communication, technology, education, science, or the arts.

God is worthy of prayer-fueled dedication. He doesn't deserve the hollow results of people living without Him. The man who began praying for the Mossis had no idea of what God intended to do through his prayers. At first, he only knew that he was supposed to pray. Then he heard God say, "Go."

Even at the end of his life, the man didn't know what God would do through the next generations of missionaries and politicians in Ouagadougou. We can only see a fraction of God's actions as we obey prayerfully.

Why would we want to make decisions based on our tiny perspectives? For our lives to go the distance and accomplish God's purposes, we need to hear, trust, and obey the One who sees it all. God can show you what to pray and the steps to find your own "Mossis." You will never see the whole picture like He does. So relax and trust God for the next step in the path He's clearing for you. By trusting God's wise and loving guidance, you can arrive at the moment when His "yoke is easy" and His "burden is light" (Matt. 11:30).

Your heart's desires can become one with God's through prayer and obedience. God's purposes come to life when we lay down our selfishness and striving. I believe God is thrilled to reveal the unique purposes He's designed for you. He's bursting with excitement as you exercise your universal callings—to go, give, communicate, and pray.

Some pray for God's will to be done in their nation or their life by asking for "more of God." It can be a sincere heart's desire to know Him better. The Holy Spirit is infinitely patient and waits for the right time for our hearts to align with His words.

If God didn't wait to speak, it would thrust us into new levels of responsibility we wouldn't be prepared for. He waits for us to pray sincerely for the Holy Spirit to purify our hearts and motives. Self-centered hearts say, "God, what is Your plan for MY life?" Purified hearts seek God simply for God. His purification is intense. We call it soul surgery or "openness and brokenness." Scripture calls it crucifying the flesh and putting to death the "old sinful man."

Seeing God face to face scared the prophet Isaiah to death. The awesome presence of God exposed sins Isaiah himself had likely forgotten.

"Woe to me! … I am ruined! For I am a man of unclean lips, and I live among a people of unclean lips, and my eyes have seen the King, the LORD Almighty."

An angel flew and touched Isaiah's unclean lips with a burning coal. The fire of heaven purified the prophet. God forgave him.

"Then I heard the voice of the Lord saying, 'Whom shall I send? And who will go for us?' And I said, 'Here am I. Send me!'" The sequence is important—Isaiah was purified first. Next, God gave the call. Then Isaiah was ready to say, "Send me!"

Jesus gave his life to give us the chance to truly live. He saves us and begins to purify the deep corruption of our lives. He inspires us by speaking out about His desires. Then, His authority is released through our obedience.

By God's grace, we can live His will. We can live His dreams. We can live His love forever.

As you continue obeying the call to pray, it will lay a foundation of trust for establishing your unique callings. It is an essential part of living God's purposes. Through listening, prayer, and careful obedience, you can go anywhere and do everything God shows you.

My prayers led me to start communicating through writing. In the remote Pacific island of Tokelau, I was astounded at how far the effect of universal callings can stretch.

No, Not Pirates

There is no way to know how far your message will go when you communicate in obedience to God. When I started writing my first book in 1983, I hadn't heard of a remote atoll called Swain's Island.

In the mid-1990s, a young Polynesian man met me after I spoke at a large outdoor gathering in New Zealand. He thanked me for teaching and explained that he was from Tokelau, a remote trio of coral islands. Tokelau is where the equator and International Date Line cross in the Pacific. Nearby is a fourth island called Swain's.

A solemn expression came upon his broad face. He softly said, "I know you get around. If someday you go to Swain's Island, would you please talk to them about returning the island to Tokelau? We don't have enough water or space on our islands, especially Fakaofa." He said the three islands of Tokelau had become dependent on New Zealand because of overcrowding and the depletion of tuna. By contrast, Swain's has many coconut trees and a rare freshwater lake. I shook the young man's large hand and answered, "If I go there, I will."

At the time, I didn't think I would ever go to Swain's Island. It had never been on my list of places to visit. It was not a dependent country, just a minor territory of American Samoa. Their population, once more than 70 people, has been as low as eight at times. The people come and go from the island, seeking further education and jobs.

About a year after the gathering service in New Zealand, my wife, kids, and I were sailing for Tokelau aboard the *Island Mercy*, a ship run by YWAM's Marine Reach ministry. A medical and dental team was also on board, ready to help the remote islanders. On the way to Tokelau, we passed near Swain's Island and dropped anchor. Swain's Island is 100 miles from the nearest landfall at Fakaofo. Three times a year, a ship anchors outside the reef, bringing supplies and mail. The island had no telephone or radio. Since we came unannounced, we alerted the Swain Islanders of our presence with a blast on the ship's horn. Soon, several came in canoes to see if we carried mail.

A group of us climbed into an inflatable dinghy and headed toward shore. The surf nudged our raft toward the Swain islanders waiting for us on the beach. They didn't look friendly, so I thought, *I hope that's a welcoming party.* We stepped off the raft onto the bright sandy beach. Then, following standard island protocol, we gave them gifts of food, books, and clothing, and our Samoan interpreter gave a speech to honor the chiefess of Swain's Island.

Our little group of YWAMers smiled at the islanders as the traditional Polynesian speech droned on. The island's head woman eyed us with great suspicion throughout the ceremony. One of our team members stood through the whole speech, holding a blue bag that contained gifts for her. She didn't seem to want it.

With the translator's help, I explained to her, "We've got a doctor, nurse, and a dentist who all want to come and minister to your people free."

I repeated, "We'll do all this for free!" But the chiefess looked quite skeptical. Her arms were stiff by her side as she stood back and listened. It was clear she didn't trust our group.

She's looking at me like I'm a pirate! She seems to have no interest in the gifts we are presenting to her.

Later, I learned that Swain's Island and Tokelau had sorrowful histories of slave ship raids during the 1800s. The slavers lured the men and boys of Swain's onto a ship under the pretense of trading for trinkets. The slave traders locked them in a hold and took them away to work in mines in Peru. Eli Jennings, an American settler who became the owner of Swain's, even colluded with the slavers who abducted islanders from Tokelau. Several times, these slavers decimated the populations of Swain's Island and Tokelau. It was no wonder she didn't trust visitors.

"What should I do, God?" I prayed.

Look in the bag.

Quickly, I rummaged through the blue bag of gifts. At the bottom, I saw a copy of one of my books. I offered it to the chiefess and had the translator explain, "I want to give you a book." I turned it over and pointed to a photo of my family on the back cover. "This is my family. They're on the ship right now," I said. "They would like to come ashore, too."

When she saw the book, her face lit up. Her 18-year-old son surprised us by speaking up in English, "We already have that book on the island!" And he ran and got a copy and asked me to sign it! I guess the book and the lack of a peg leg proved we weren't pirates! After that, the Swain's residents welcomed my family and the team onto the island.

It has amazed me to see how far that book has traveled. After reading it, kings and government leaders have invited me to meet with them. There is no limit to how far you can communicate when you do it in God's will. Whether you speak like me, write it like my sister, Janice, or translate like my other sister, Phyllis, we all have a call to tell the gospel. Through praying, going, giving, and communicating, we bring God's peace and salvation to the very ends of the earth.

As my family and others on our team came ashore, we noticed only a handful of residents on that beautiful atoll. The island's rainfall has made the land-locked lagoon into a freshwater lake. Around it were as many coconut trees as could be packed onto that mile-long island.

The people invited me to speak at the little church they had on the island. While there, I met a young woman from the Jennings family. She had inherited ownership of the island.

"I'm not sure I want to live here forever," she told me. It was understandable, given the island's extreme seclusion. I had not forgotten the Tokalauan man in New Zealand. So I told her the young man's request.

I asked, "Would you please consider giving this island back to Tokelau?"

I knew it was a big request. She could sell the island for millions. Miss Jennings told me she was a believer and would pray about it. I don't know the result of my appeal for Tokelau. But in that moment, I sensed God working as I echoed the plea of that young man in New Zealand.

You won't always witness the results when you obey God and communicate in His will. Sometimes, people accept His words with joy and thanks, like they did on Swain's Island. Other times, you'll be rejected or even physically attacked for communicating the message of God. Paul understood this well. He told Timothy he was suffering because he brought the gospel. "I am suffering even to the point of being chained like a criminal," he lamented. "But God's word is not chained" (2 Tim 2:8,9).

God's truth is without borders. His words are without boundaries. Nothing can "chain" a message from Him.

NORTH AFRICAN INTERROGATION

It is my personal mission to physically "Go into all the world"[42] to open doors for other missionaries. In my lifetime, the dawn of airline travel has made it possible to reach places once considered impossible to access. Years ago, I determined to go to all nations as Christ's ambassador, and though physical barriers have come down, some political ones remain.

For decades, I had no legal way to follow God's call to go to every country. The hardest to enter was Libya. U.S. sanctions and Libyan law made it illegal even to try. Libya was refusing my visa requests.

I prayed about what to do and decided to try to gain access to Libya's North African neighbors, Tunisia and Algeria. I booked an airline ticket to Tunisia, then would drive southwest to a more remote border access point on the Libya-Algeria border.

Before the trip, I had surgery to remove my gallbladder and appendix. A ventral hernia developed after surgeons sewed up the 11-inch (28 cm) incision. It looked like a bump protruding from my abdomen. Corrective surgery was scheduled in California, but first, I would go through Tunisia and try for Algeria. Algeria was nearly as dangerous to enter as Libya, but if I could get in, it might get me a step closer to finishing my call. I rented a compact car at Camelcar car rental agency in Tunis,

---

42. Mark 16:17 NKJV

then navigated miles of empty roadway toward the Algerian border. As I drove, I prayed silently for God's protection and direction. *Show me what to do, Lord. I respect the rulers and authorities you've placed, but I respect You most of all. Lead me, Lord.*

God prompted me to check my jacket pocket. In it was a shekel from a past trip to Israel.

Better get rid of this! I parked and tossed it away.

When the border appeared, I slowed the car, trying not to arouse suspicion. I hoped the Tunisian guards might wave me through to Algeria. But one guard strutted to the car and ordered, "Get out."

I forced a smile as he sternly pointed for me to go inside. There was no choice but to go in. I moved carefully with my bags, minding my hernia. One man was assigned to inspect the baggage. Even before opening the bags, he looked upset. The man pointed at my papers and shouted something in Arabic. Another man motioned to me to his desk. "Show me documents now!"

I produced my American passport and tried to smile outwardly. Inside, I was praying hard, "God, open the door. Help me get through!"

Seeing the US passport, the guard reached for his radio and alerted his commander. Soon, a tall man wearing sunglasses and an officer's uniform began questioning me.

"What is your purpose for coming to Tunisia?" he barked in English.

"To get to see North Africa," I answered.

The interrogator waved his finger repeatedly like he was scolding a child. "We will not tolerate any lies from you. Again, what is your reason for coming to Tunisia?"

"Sir, I just wanted to see this part of North Africa," I replied.

"You are a Jew, aren't you?" the man sneered. "You are a spy from Israel, trying to sneak into our country."

As I exhaled slowly, my hand brushed the now-empty jacket pocket.

He stared down with cold hatred. "You really speak Arabic, I know. You pretend to speak only English. But I know you speak our language!"

"All I know is '*shokran*,'"[43] I said with my American accent.

Through the door on the left, I saw men searching through my rental car. The first interrogator was replaced with another and then another as hours dragged on. By the end, six men took turns blasting me with accusations.

"You are married to an Israeli, aren't you?" one angry interrogator slammed his fist onto the counter. "Your wife is a Jew."

"No, she is a blonde, born in Canada, and now an American," I answered, not giving any more information than I had to.

He pointed in my face. "I know you are married to a Jew woman," he spat.

Outside, I saw a white car arrive with a driver and the commander in his dark sunglasses. They exited the vehicle and left its door standing wide open.

Oh, no! They're going to take me somewhere.

The commander strode in confidently and interrupted the interrogator with sharp orders in Arabic. He turned toward me and said, "For the very last time, I ask you, why are you really in Tunisia?"

As I prayed silently, an idea came. "I'll show you," I turned to face him.

"What?" the commander asked.

"Look here." I unzipped the jacket and pressed down my knit shirt, revealing the bulge of the ventral hernia in my abdomen. "You see, I am not well. Next week, I will have surgery at a hospital in America. Anything could happen in surgery. I only

43. Shokran is "thank you" in Arabic

wanted to see North Africa first," I said with a wince, zipping my jacket again.

The interrogator's eyes widened in astonishment. He must have wondered, "What is this man doing here in this condition? If he dies here, I'll be in trouble."

The main interrogator rubbed his neck while looking in my direction. "OK, you may enter Algeria," he said.

"Oh, I think I had better return to Tunis," I answered the commander.

It would be foolish to risk this again and not be able to get out of Algeria.

With relief, I gathered my bags and went to the car. Without looking back, I shut the door and sped away. Though I didn't get through as I'd hoped, I had learned what I needed to know. Algeria was not an option then. I navigated my way back through Tunisia, realizing what I just escaped.

The Only Safety

They could have imprisoned me when I tried to cross into Algeria. God protected me instead. It is hard to say why the Lord works the way He does. Only God knows precisely how and why He acts on our behalf. Hebrews 11 commends the ones who "escaped the edge of the sword; whose weakness was turned to strength; and who became powerful in battle and routed foreign armies."[44] Their faith was answered with protection and grace to overcome.

Yet the chapter goes on to describe many faithful men and women of God who faced imprisonment, torture, and death. These "destitute, persecuted and mistreated" believers are also commended for their faith.

It seems unfair to see some believers persecuted and others protected. But God isn't missing in times of danger. He knows

---

44. Hebrews 11:34

NORTH AFRICAN INTERROGATION   91

when we need the grace to stand in the fire like Shadrach, Meshach, and Abednego did. Under threat of death, they said that God "will rescue us from your hand, O king. But even if he does not, we want you to know, O king, that we will not serve your gods…"[45]

The Babylonian king ordered the petroleum-fueled furnace to be heated seven times hotter than for regular executions. Executioners got burned alive as they threw the young Israelites into the furnace.

But then the king was shocked to see "one who looks like a son of the gods" with them in the flames. The Son stands with us in suffering. True safety is knowing we will be with Jesus, no matter the sacrifice. With Him, we can face the furnace and any risks ahead. I realized this more clearly during a road race on the Pan-American highway.

High-Speed Highway Chase

I bought a new yellow school bus for a mission to Central America. Installing an extra gas tank and a toilet prepared the bus to drive 700 miles non-stop on the Pan-American highway.

As our team headed back to Texas and California from Nicaragua, we stopped in El Salvador to fill the gas tanks before crossing into Guatemala. I'd heard a civil war was starting in Guatemala, but I had no idea how bad it had become. At the border, officials stopped us. The rest of the 40 riding on the bus were asleep.

Among the team aboard, we had the 19-year-old nephew of a famous governor of Guatemala. After a while, they came and demanded all the passports. So, we gave them.

"Stay in the bus," they ordered.

We watched and waited while the officials didn't budge. Without words, the men's nods and gestures told me everything.

45. Daniel 3:17-18

They expected a bribe. I don't pay bribes. So, I tried to pay whatever legitimate fee might be needed. But there was none.

The conversation dragged on for 45 minutes till the governor's nephew came up and said, "Can I get out?"

Maybe he wants to use a restroom or get food inside?

He went inside and suddenly came out with the entire team's passports.

"How did you get them?" I stared in surprise.

"I told them who I was," he answered. "They immediately handed over the passports."

Oh, no. If they are with the rebel faction, they may come after us!

We headed back out. As I feared, 45 minutes down that long, straight road, we spotted a roadblock. A man was standing, holding up his arms in the center of the highway. Three others stood on the side of the road by a Jeepster wagon. Seeing the men, I knew something was off. So, I hit the gas. I was coming at him at 60, then 70 miles an hour. Then we blew past him.

The Jeepster began chasing us down the highway. They revved their engine, trying to get around us. But with the bulk of our big bus, I swerved, blocking them from getting close enough to shoot.

After a long run on the straightaway, I approached a narrow road winding into the mountains. In a roadside service station, I spotted a powder blue station wagon pulling out to block our lane. With the first car behind us and another in front, I kept up my speed, even forcing oncoming traffic off the road.

We now had both the Jeepster and the blue wagon chasing us up the narrow road! Revving through the mountain's turns, I kept our bus just ahead of them. Whenever they tried to get past us, I would swerve to block them again and again, on and on, till we got away.

The bus' extra gas tank let us outlast our pursuers. Both cars had to finally give up while we rolled to the relative safety of Guatemala City.

We refueled and dropped off some teammates with mission contacts there. "Thank God you didn't stop!" our friends exclaimed. "Yesterday, that rebel group stopped a bus. They robbed and shot everyone!"

They warned that to get out of Guatemala, we would have to drive across a long one-way bridge over a river chasm in rebel-controlled territory. If we didn't cross over the border bridge before 6 p.m., getting out of the country now in full civil war would be impossible.

Racing against the clock, I kept a fast pace all the way to the bridge. Our bus crossed into Mexico with only five minutes to spare!

I finally stepped down from the big bus, grateful to be okay. Slumping onto the curb, I took a minute to recover from the spent adrenaline. Then, bam! Bam! Bullets started flying over my head!

I ducked behind a concrete pillar beside a Mexican guard. "Que paso, hombre?!" I asked him (what's going on?).

He shrugged. "That? That's the war. At 6 p.m., they always start shooting, even across the border."

In a lull of the shooting, we pulled away from the rebel territory, grateful for the calm of Mexico.

When Christ Divides

Living God's will can mean defying authorities, peers, and family. Jesus said, "Don't imagine that I came to bring peace to the earth! I came not to bring peace but a sword. 'I have come to set a man against his father, a daughter against her mother, and a daughter-in-law against her mother-in-law. Your enemies will be right in your own household!'"[46]

It is confusing to hear this from Jesus. He valued family. Some of His last words from the cross were instructions for

46. Matthew 10:34-36 NLT

John to care for Mary, Jesus' mother. His teachings defend marriage and call us to honor our parents. Remembering this helps us realize what Jesus meant by saying He will divide families.

Jesus was describing what happens when part of a family accepts Him as Lord while others don't. If you start answering to God first, it destroys some "normal" ways of operating between you and your parents, teachers, friends, and other authorities. Many people won't understand when God becomes your heavenly father, teacher, friend, and authority.

Those who know Him as Lord and Master will get it. They will probably even relate more closely to you. The ones who disapprove will try to help get you back in line with their expectations. Most want what they believe is best for you. They'll offer rewards of help, opportunities, and approval. But each of the rewards will have strings of expectation attached.

Some will try to influence through penalties like disapproval, rejection, or other punishments. It'll be very personal. One of our young worker's parents told him, "We'd rather you be a drug addict than a missionary."

Most of the world is controlled by these types of punishments and rewards. The lowest of these are threats and bribes. Corruption by threats and bribery isn't just in local and national governments. It targets our work, education, and family. How will our actions be governed? By civilized incentives and self-interest? By threat and bribe? Or by God's word and a holy will to live differently?

Our world has been threatened and bribed into what is now "normal." To change the world, we must be ready to reject bribes. We also must be willing to receive unreasonable punishments for our godly actions. It isn't fair. It is real.

BEYOND NATURE AND NURTURE

God cares deeply about the suffering of the world. As you follow Him, you'll be praying new prayers and taking action to address the problems of the hurting people around you. Many of the world's greatest problems aren't natural. Pollution, crime, and war generally come from misguided human behavior.

Scientists have spent decades studying what motivates human behavior in hopes of understanding and lessening the suffering people cause. Psychologists have long debated whether people are the product of environment, genetics, or both. They agree that DNA profoundly affects your body, personality, and intelligence. Still, this is only part of the picture.

The environment we grow up in—be it positive or negative—brings to bear a significant influence on behavior. Children who grow up with supportive parents and a sense of health and safety succeed in life much better than those who suffer parental abuse or neglect. Researchers have studied the behavior of rats to learn more about the effects of their environment. The rats receive food rewards for navigating a maze or pressing the correct buttons. The rats receive electric shocks or other negative reinforcements to teach them what not to do. These train or "condition" rats for experiments with genetic modifications, electronic implants, and other scientific studies.

Conditioning human behavior is now a popular idea to fix society's urgent problems. For most people, conditioning does work. For the majority, nothing is more important than comfort and self-preservation. Fascist and communist governments adopted conditioning techniques to channel aggression towards dissidents and exercise control over the media and other vital parts of society. The threat of violence is a potent tool for leaders who wish to control nations like scientists control rats. Whole countries are brought to heel by the mass murder of citizens who violate their controlling laws.

Good governments also enforce laws to help control people's criminal intentions but usually use humane methods. Even the best prisons cannot stop criminal intent; they can only contain it. Even perfectly controlled prisons cannot reform all criminals.

It is right to punish lawbreakers and encourage good behavior. Of all people, believers should be the quickest to obey the laws of governments, whether there is a threat of punishment or not. We should respect teachers, police, pastors, and government officials. We should be the first to honor our fathers and mothers. Of course, we answer to an even higher law. Who do you obey if your parents say "don't" and God says "do"? Who do you obey if your government says "stop" and God's Word says "go"?

The one you obey is your real lord and master. This is why Jesus said He did not come to bring peace. This is also why many communists and fascists attack believers. They think they can control you through threats and bribes.

Even countries with the most civilized governments in the world encourage immorality. Sophisticated modern nations have medical and governmental policies that promote euthanasia, abortion, and the creation of embryos for manipulation and destruction in scientific research. How many souls will they sacrifice to secure health or wealth? As God's people, we must not be manipulated by the media's influence, popular opinion, or government policies that provide civilized incentives to sin.

If you "resisted sin to the point of shedding your blood,"[47] the authorities would realize they cannot manipulate you. You can live above the manipulation of your environment. With Christ as Lord, you won't be lawless or corrupt. Instead, by the Holy Spirit, you can have the fruit of self-control.[48]

The only time any follower of Jesus should break a law is if it contradicts the law of the Bible. Paul wrote, "Remind the believers to submit to the government and its officers. They should be obedient, always ready to do what is good.»[49]

Nero, the Roman Caesar who later murdered many believers, was Paul's ruler during the writing of this passage. Paul knew how difficult it was to be subject to rulers and authorities. In Acts, Paul's legal defense before the Roman rulers, Felix, Festus, and Agrippa, shows that he practiced what he preached. He did not seek to subvert their laws or authority. Paul simply defended his rights by law.

And so, the followers of Jesus must also be subject to the law. Even if there were no laws, scripture says that those who belong to Christ Jesus will be guided by the fruit of the Spirit, "love, joy, peace, patience, kindness, goodness, faithfulness, gentleness, and self-control.[50]»

Law is insufficient when people do not have the fruit of God's Spirit. Legal incentives, powerful threats, and bribes are never enough to control everyone fully. There is an element of our humanity that doesn't come from DNA or environment. Good or bad, people yearn for the freedom to choose what they will do with their life. To be truly free means to be free of the addiction of sin. You cannot achieve this through law alone. Something greater must guide and redeem our hearts and minds.

---

47. Hebrews 12:2
48. Galatians 5:23 NLT
49. Titus 3:1 NLT
50. Galatians 5

Legalism cannot change us like love. "For the Lord is the Spirit, and wherever the Spirit of the Lord is, there is freedom.[51]"

Tragically, many people reduce the Bible to a list of rules, rewards, and punishments. This is probably the lowest understanding of God's word. To use heaven like a bribe and hell like a threat misses God's desire.

Jesus lived and died so we can learn love. God's love means choosing the highest good for others and yourself. His love teaches us what it means to be believers. A gospel of threat and bribe is a grotesque distortion of God's message because it doesn't teach the love of Jesus.

Without God, reality is hell, whether now or in eternity. With God, eternal life begins. In relationship with God, we learn the real meaning of eternal life. "This is eternal life: that they may know you, the only true God, and Jesus Christ, whom you have sent.[52]"

This message of eternity is nearly impossible to understand or believe without messengers who live it.

So, we must be beyond the influence of threats and bribes if we expect our message to be believed. We can't live like rats in cages while singing of hope and liberty. We must be free of the cowardice and greed that cages so many. They can't believe a message we can't live. But by God's grace, we can live it.

To live God's purposes for me, I realized I would have to get into Libya soon. There still weren't any safe ways to go in. There weren't any legal ways into the country either. It didn't matter that I'd been on missions to 237 countries. If I failed to enter Libya, I would not have obeyed the call God gave me when I was 13. I couldn't please both God and the Libyan government. It was clear. I had to go, whether the powers and authorities agreed or not.

---

51. 2 Corinthians 3:17 NLT
52. John 17 NLT

LAID LOW IN TUNISIA

Throughout the 1990s, Americans were prohibited from entering Libya—especially without visas. My first overland attempt had given me a stark reminder of how dangerous it was for an American missionary to travel in North Africa. By 1995, I was nearly 60 and felt a growing urgency to get into Libya. That spring, an Arabic friend named Azim[53] agreed to travel with me and translate on my second overland border attempt.

I flew into Tunisia again to try to drive directly to the eastern border with Libya. All the tourists and other visitors seemed to pass security inspection at the Tunis airport effortlessly. But as soon as the officer entered my passport into the computer, he singled me out for special inspection. No one said a word—but I knew I was flagged because of my earlier attempt to pass through Tunisia. I was questioned again, but the officers soon released me, and I hired a taxi to take me to a hotel.

Leaving the airport, a white SUV carrying men I presumed to be secret police followed us. At the hotel I tried to call Switzerland, but in the background I could hear surveillance agents talking. *I guess I'm not alone!*

The next morning, I went to meet Azim at the airport. The same SUV began tailing us as we pulled away from the hotel.

Wait! I have an idea.

"Take me back to the airport entrance, please," I told the taxi driver. As we pulled into the entrance, the men gave up tailing us.

---

53. Real name withheld for safety

They must have assumed I was flying home!

Relieved, I went inside and found Azim. I rented a little hatchback car, and we loaded our bags. We pulled out of the airport together, heading for the open road. No one followed as we pushed toward the Libyan border.

Out on a lonely road surrounded by desert sands, one of the tires began to thump. We stopped and found the tire flat. Azim located a spare tire in the trunk, and I started pumping the jack to raise the car.

The North African sun shone brightly on the sand piled beside the road. When we replaced the tire, I lifted the flat and carried it to the back of the car. With my right arm, I began to pitch it into the trunk. The instant I let go, I felt a wrenching in my lower spine.

"Oh, no," my eyes squeezed shut as the pain ripped through me. The tire thudded into the trunk.

"Are you OK, Loren?" Azim asked.

"I hope so," I answered while rubbing my back. Since 1964, I have struggled with my back injury when our van rolled in the desert of Arizona.[54]

I eased myself behind the steering wheel, and we got rolling again. Mile-by-mile, my back was getting worse. It felt like fire was spreading from my lower back to my whole body. I struggled to concentrate on driving as we neared the border.

"I'm sorry. I can't keep going, Azim. My back is really hurt," I said. "Let's turn in at the next town."

After driving the last twelve minutes, Azim spotted a modest hotel. Pulling up to the curb, I struggled to get out of the car. When I tried to straighten up, I nearly fell over. Waves of pain hit me with every step.

---

54. Read more on this incident in *Making Jesus Lord,* by Loren Cunningham with Janice Rogers

"Please…ask the hotel worker…get a piece of plywood to put on my bed. Ooohh…" I clenched my teeth as another shock of pain hit me. "I have got to lie down flat."

"I will call a doctor, too," Azim answered.

The local doctor was able to help with some muscle relaxers and anti-inflammatory pain medication. But we stayed three nights, and my condition wasn't improving.

"Go…into all the world," the bold image I'd seen decades before, was as immediate as ever. I didn't want to let Satan or anything keep me from obeying God. By human reasoning, I should have been looking for a way out of there. Instead, my thoughts and emotions wrapped around the mission God gave me. Azim went to the border to see what he could learn. When he returned, he said, "Loren, I am sorry to report that troops are massing at the border. At first, I thought this was war! But no, it is a military exercise."

I discussed with him the idea of going by camel caravan, helicopter, or boat, but those ideas also failed. While he was out searching for possible routes, I went to prayer. "God, I don't understand. Is this the enemy trying to stop us? Azim and I are doing what we can. Is there something we missed? Is there something You want me to learn? I really don't get it. Why bring me this far and not let me go in, Lord?"

By the time Azim returned, I'd been praying for over an hour. He looked at me and shook his head. He was concerned we could be arrested for trying to enter by sea without a visa. "I am very sorry," Azim sank onto his bed.

"Okay, Azim. Thank you for trying,"

Inside, my thoughts were still churning. I closed my eyes again and focused on God.

Lord, are You blocking me?

I waited solemnly and listened for God. "Yes. Now get up and go home," God answered.

My eyes opened wide with surprise. *This crisis was God stopping us!* Azim's eyes turned to me as I moved to the edge of the bed. Setting my feet down squarely on the ground, I started to push myself upward.

"Loren!" Azim was shocked to see me rising so quickly. I stood up straight for the first time in three days. A broad smile appeared when I realized the pain had subsided! My back wasn't swollen anymore.

Azim watched in surprise as I got my shirt on and prepared to leave. "God's blocking us," I said. "He told me to go home."

"Home?" Azim asked.

"Yeah, we're going back," I said while walking toward the car. We checked out and drove the long road back to Tunis Airport. I made it to my plane without trouble. There weren't even any special searches from the inspectors. I was back home in Switzerland by noon. A youth rally had their keynote speaker canceled, so I was just in time to preach to 1,200 young people. When I finally got home, I sat down with Darlene to pray.

"God, why did you have me go if I wasn't going to get in?" I asked.

After listening to the Lord, I opened my eyes and turned to Dar. "God said, 'I wanted to test you to see if you were still willing to go to prison for me.' And I passed the test."

Dar smiled and said, "I believe God is going to get you in the front door!"

The front door with a legal visa. A true answer to prayer!

The next day, I took the long flights to Bhutan to meet secretly with Christian leaders. My back was fine throughout the plane flights and the rough roads of Bhutan. I was safe and well again. But I'd been kept out of Libya a second time. The door remained firmly shut.

Some doors stay closed for a very long time. After God told Abraham to "Go to a land I will show you" (Gen 12:1), it took hundreds of years until the Israelites arrived and took possession of their promised land.

Recalling Abraham and some of the Bible's greatest heroes of faith, Hebrews says there were ones who "pleased God because of their faith! But still, they died without being given what had been promised." (Heb. 11:39 CEV)

Some things God tells us to go and do cannot be done in a lifetime. After the close calls I'd had, some wondered if I would ever make it to Libya in this lifetime. Looking back on that painful injury, I see God was testing me. I could have failed Him. There were strong reasons to quit—the injury, the danger, and the laws that barricaded my way.

I don't have answers for why I reacted the way I did during that injury. I was not looking for a way out but a way forward. It is difficult to describe, but there are times when your every thought and action can be fixed on God's purposes.

It is God's grace. Like in a slow-motion movie sequence, you experience a total awareness of what you're supposed to do. God's grace can allow you to do things that would be impossible otherwise. The usual distractions, temptations, and fears go dim as God's path lights up before you.

I don't always feel this, and I cannot make it happen. The sporadic times I have experienced this grace were when I actively obeyed God's purposes. The grace was only there when I absolutely needed it to do what He'd shown me. Like that grace, many of God's ways are only apparent while living His purposes.

That agonizing time in the desert taught me that, but Libya had eluded me again. Still, I knew God's light was on my path. I knew I would go to Libya soon.

LIBYA, MY FINAL BORDER

In the late 1990s, Qaddafi still ruled Libya with fierce dominance. The United States 1998 Global Terrorism Overview listed Libya as one of five nations involved in state-sponsored terrorism. Because of their open support for Palestinian terrorists, the United Nations and the U.S. were choking Libya's economy with trade sanctions and other financial penalties.

With travel to Libya still out of reach, I called a friend serving in the British House of Lords. "Is there any way to get into Libya now?" I asked. He said he would try.

He called back a few days later. "Loren, the Libyan government has rejected your latest request. I don't know what else you can do about getting into the country."

So I waited and prayed. There was no change in Libya's isolation until April 5, 1999, when its government finally handed over the suspects from the Pan Am flight that exploded over Lockerbie, Scotland, in 1988. The accused were to stand trial in the Netherlands. The United Nations lifted sanctions after this move by the Libyan government. Then, Britain quickly renewed their diplomatic relations with Libya.

From my home in Switzerland, I anxiously watched every news report on Libya. I made a call to the Libyan embassy in Switzerland. For the first time, they were able to help me. I was put in contact with a travel agent willing to "sponsor" my visit to Libya. After all these years of attempts and disappointments, I tried not to get my hopes too high.

Two YWAM workers, Magdy from the Middle East and Markus from Europe, agreed to go with me to Libya. It would be a team of three. At the YWAM campus in Lausanne, we told the staff and students about our trip so they could support us with prayer. As we gathered to pray for Libya, one young woman from Colombia said God had given her a vision. She saw three strands of a necklace linked together. One strand broke and fell to the ground. She said, "Magdy, I believe you are the strand that could fall." We all understood that we were to pray especially hard for Magdy. It made sense—as a Middle Eastern believer, he was more vulnerable than Markus or me.

The Cost of His Cause

Even with a visa and ticket in hand, I knew I wouldn't make it to Libya without God's help. The country had been in the grip of a brutal dictator for thirty years. In 1998, the United Nations reported "persistent allegations of systematic use of torture and cruel, inhuman or degrading treatment or punishment." It was a dark time for Libya. I knew our prayers were crucial.

To live God's purposes, you often must confront people and spirits who are resisting God. The darkness you'll encounter is often entrenched in government, entertainment, education, or science. If you live God's purposes, you will face opposition from authorities in every area of society, even from religion.

Jesus' greatest opposition did not come from the Roman authorities. It came from the religious leaders. Jesus broke their legalistic interpretations of God's laws about the Sabbath, Gentiles, disease (leprosy), and capital punishment (the adulteress in John 8). He broke the letter of the law while upholding the spirit of the law. It infuriated the Pharisees and Sadducees, who brought false charges against Jesus. Their lies took His life.

So, we must give our lives to God's purposes without reserve. We cannot live like Jesus without being willing to die like Him. As you pray for God's will, ask God to examine your own will. Ask Him, "Am I willing to pay the price?"

If you break a law, tradition, or cultural practice, be ready to face punishment. It does not matter if you violate a law from a godly motivation. You'll still have to pay the consequences.

When Jesus faced Pilate, he didn't defend himself. Astonished, Pilate said, "Don't you realize I have power either to free you or to crucify you?"

"You would have no power over me if it were not given to you from above," Jesus replied. By this, Jesus could be implying that as a governor, Pilate possessed the authority to execute him.

God led many spiritual leaders to break rules, even His rules. Ezekiel ate "unclean food." Paul opposed the ones teaching Gentiles to be circumcised. God even told the prophet Isaiah to protest Israel's alliance with Egypt by being naked in the royal court for years[55]!

Once they know God's will, prophets and apostles prepare for sacrifice. Already imprisoned, Jeremiah bought a field in enemy territory. Paul returned to Jerusalem, knowing he faced persecution[56]. Except for John, all the original apostles died for their faith.

Yet John also paid the price for Christ. *Fox's Book of Martyrs* provides an early church account[57]. "From Ephesus, he was sent to Rome, where he was cast into a cauldron of boiling oil. He escaped by miracle, without injury."

Stephen courageously faced death, saying, "You are just like your fathers: You always resist the Holy Spirit! Was there ever a prophet your fathers did not persecute? They even killed those who predicted the coming of the Righteous One. And now you have betrayed and murdered him....[58]»

---

55. Isaiah 20
56. Acts 21:13
57. Foxes Book of Martyrs - Chapter 1
58. Acts 7:51, 52

Stephen paid the price. Our YWAM missionaries are paying the price more and more as the days grow darker. To live like Jesus, we must be ready to do the same.

Discerning and Overcoming

The confrontations I had already faced in North Africa convinced me there were more than just people opposing this plan to enter Libya. The fear and violence in Libya at that time were diabolical.

I needed to learn how to overcome this kind of opposition. For me, the two most important things are spiritually discerning what is happening and confronting it in an opposite manner.

Spiritual discernment is when you recognize something spiritual is going on. It could be something specific, like knowing exactly how to pray for someone with a spirit of suicide. It is also possible to discern something more general, like experiencing the Holy Spirit or sensing a demonic presence. If you keep hitting long-standing obstacles, ask God for discernment. Ask Him to show you if you've given away authority by giving in to sin. He will answer and restore you as you seek Him sincerely.

When we were praying for Libya and our Colombian friend Rachel heard from God that Magdy would be attacked, we knew to pay attention to that warning. Once in Libya, we prayed daily for discernment about how the enemy would try to stop Magdy.

The second important element is confronting the enemy in an opposite spirit. Throughout Jesus' life, He would do and say things opposite of what people expected.

He asked the rich young ruler to sell all he owned. This man expected a reward for his piety, but he was challenged to be free of greed.

Jesus met a man possessed by demons and asked, "What is your name?" The demons answered with a number, not a name.

They said we are "Legion, for we are many." Roman legions were in the thousands. No one could chain him. Jesus gave him true freedom with a calm word, treating the possessed man with dignity and personal care.

Jesus knew exactly how to silence the powerful and stir people from apathy.

"...Pray for those who mistreat you. If someone strikes you on one cheek, turn to him the other also," Jesus taught.

He was explaining how to act in ways that are opposite to the ways of the world. The same principle behind turning the other cheek is also at work when we live God's purposes. It is how to act as well as react in an opposite manner.

God's purposes are attainable as you discern the enemy's tactics and act in an opposite spirit. Instead of trying to "fight fire with fire," we must follow Jesus' example and work in the opposite spirit.

In Libya, that would mean opposing intimidation with peaceful kindness. If we faced injustice, we would have to act with grace to overcome it.

THROUGH LIBYA'S
FRONT DOOR

We finished our preparations that morning. Then, we boarded an airplane from Zurich heading south to Tripoli, Libya. After all I'd been through on earlier attempts, it almost seemed too easy to have a visa and fly in on a spacious Airbus with Swiss Air. But there I was, just days after getting permission to enter the country. At the airport in Tripoli, I was standing in line with my two friends, waiting for an official to give our passports the stamp of Libya.

A lifetime's memories poured through my thoughts as the reality sank in—I had made it! Hushed groups of Libyans passed through inspection briskly. The amber-eyed youth I noticed earlier was watching the line of arrivals.

We had to wait for the officials to finish reviewing our documents. One official eyed me carefully while flipping through the pages of my passport. He keyed my passport information into the computer and pointed me toward another line for foreign visitors.

Magdy, Markus, and I went forward in line to meet a stern-looking guard who began saying something forcefully in Arabic. Magdy's head fell in shock as the guard shouted his harsh instructions. Then Magdy answered with what sounded like a protest in Arabic.

The guard sternly pointed at a sign that said "exchange." The teenage boy who was watching the line saw the outburst and fled.

"What's going on?" I asked Magdy.

"He wants us each to change $1,000 into Libyan dinars," Magdy pointed at a sign they had posted. "But look at this exchange rate! It is a trick. They are stealing most of our money if we do it. Besides, we don't even have $3,000."

The official started raising his voice again and demanded we exchange the money. Magdy answered as politely as possible yet resisted the man's demands for the exchange. At that, the official repeated Magdy's last words, yelling them louder and louder.

Magdy blanched at the guard's rage. Markus and I looked at each other as if to say, *Now what?*

The official continued his ranting in Arabic and began pointing back at the airplane we'd come in. *Does he mean to send Magdy back!?* But then Magdy bounced back with a confident smile and a calm tone. He nodded at the man and pointed to the exchange booth.

Stepping over to us, Magdy asked, "What can we do? Do we have $1,000 to exchange?"

After a quick count, we realized there was only enough for one of us. I thought back to Rachel's vision of the third broken strand. *Our third strand is falling.*

I looked at him and whispered, "Apologize to him, and we will pray." Magdy walked slowly up to the man and began to apologize in Arabic. His hands were held out slightly, requesting the official's pardon. Markus and I prayed silently.

The guard nodded his head, accepting Magdy's words. I breathed out slowly with relief. We exchanged the money we had, and the official sent us on through customs without further incident.

As we left the inspection area, I asked Magdy, "What was that guy so angry about?"

"Well, when he told me to exchange the money for that ridiculous rate, I said, 'But this is unfair.' Only the Arabic word for 'unfair' is stronger than in English. In Arabic, it means something like: 'You are breaking God's command.' So he was yelling and asking, 'Are you coming here to teach us what is fair or not fair?'"

"I see… what did you say that calmed him?" I asked Magdy as we continued walking towards the waiting area.

Magdy smiled again, "I apologized and said, 'You and I are Arabic brothers. Please, I did not mean to insult you.'"

Arriving at the waiting area, Magdy stopped and said, "The man told me, 'Yes, we are Arabic brothers. Only these other two must exchange 500.'"

"Ahh, *that's* how we got through," I said as we sat together in the empty waiting area. The three of us arranged our bags and began waiting for the travel agent who had sponsored our visas. The Libyan government used these sponsors, or guides, as a pretense to spy on every new visitor. No one could freely walk around their nation without one of these sponsors accompanying them.

After a while, I checked my watch. An hour had already passed since we'd arrived. The travel agent was still nowhere to be seen. *Perhaps that teen watching the line warned his father, the agent, not to come?*

"Let's go," I said. "I bet the problem with that official scared our sponsor off. Besides, without him watching us, we'll be able to do more anyway."

We loaded our bags into a taxi and headed to the hotel the travel agent had reserved. At the front desk, Magdy spoke in English to the hotel manager, "Hello. We have a reservation for three under the name of Magdy Khaleem. May we check in?"

The manager looked over the reservations for some time before looking up, "I am sorry, sir, but there seems to be no reservation under this name. Are you certain this was the correct hotel and reservation?"

"Yes, it is," Magdy answered. "I am positive."

"I am sorry, but there is no reservation, and our rooms are full," the man shrugged.

I motioned for Magdy to come close. "Maybe the agent was afraid and canceled our reservation. Let's go to another hotel."

We hailed a taxi and went searching for another hotel. After finding one with a vacancy, we checked in. We went out to the balcony to talk. I'd been warned that the Libyan secret police bugged every hotel room.

"This is much better to be here and not have to worry about the sponsor," I said to the guys.

Markus agreed, "Since we're at a different hotel, the government probably doesn't know where we are."

"You should have seen what the newspaper said at the airport!" Magdy said.

"What was it?" Markus asked.

"The headlines were crazy. It said that the world was applauding Qaddafi for negotiating peace in Yugoslavia. Ridiculous!" Magdy said.

"Qaddafi's propaganda," I remarked with a chuckle. "Let's go find some dinner."

Together, we began walking the twilight streets of Tripoli in search of a restaurant. While walking down a darkened sidewalk, Markus and I were talking. About a block away, a car sped through an intersection and was racing toward us. Suddenly, Markus fell into a three-foot-deep hole beside the road! As Markus fell, his momentum took him toward the street. The car kept speeding, heading straight toward the hole. In an instant, it zoomed by where Markus had fallen. It missed his head by only a few inches.

"I'm okay!" Markus exclaimed with a laugh. Magdy helped him up.

"It's amazing that my momentum didn't throw me into the car. Thank God, I landed perfectly on both feet!"

The following day, we went to breakfast at the hotel restaurant. With the exchange rate we'd paid at the airport, the breakfast cost an equivalent of $127. That was just for one piece of bread, a banana, an egg, and a cup of tea. We gave thanks and ate it together. The only way we could make the dinar currency go further was by eating less. Exchanging money with a black-market money trader was out of the question.

Later that day, Magdy told me about how a man living there in Tripoli, Azwari[59], came to meet him. Magdy told me he'd asked Azwari if he knew Youth With A Mission. When the visitor said yes, Magdy asked, "Do you know who the founder is?"

When Azwari answered yes, Magdy said, "Well, he is here upstairs."

"How did he get in? This is impossible!" Azwari whispered back to Magdy.

They quickly left the hotel to avoid being overheard. Magdy explained things and arranged to meet Azwari the next day at the Roman ruins in Sabrata.

In the morning, our team stood together in the ancient ruins of a Roman theater. We listened as Azwari told us about Libya, "There are three important things for us growing up in Libya: food, drink and fear. Libya has been controlled for centuries. The Greeks, Romans, Byzantines, and Italians all ruled over Libya. And now we have Qaddafi."

The following day, we were to meet Azwari near a hospital. I took out a little camera and started to get a few pictures of the buildings when Azwari drove by and yelled out his car window, "Meet me around the corner!"

We walked around the corner to the place he'd parked. Before even greeting us, Azwar warned us, "Do not ever be

59. name changed for safety

taking pictures like that here!" As we drove away, he explained. "It is illegal to take photos in non-designated places. The sponsor is supposed to show you where it is legal to take pictures."

I was surprised we still hadn't seen or heard anything from the sponsor who was supposed to guide us. We drove around Tripoli and prayed for God's will to be done in every area of society—business, education, church, media, art, family, science, and government.

We passed by an old cathedral erected by the Italians. "The only Libyans allowed to attend churches are the secret police. They go to every meeting. This cathedral is now used to train Islamic missionaries to go all over the world."

Azwari drove us in front of an empty lot in a suburb of Tripoli. "One of Qaddafi's head officials didn't even disagree with him—he only added a suggestion to Qaddafi's instructions. For that, he was killed, and his villa was bulldozed before his family could even get their belongings. The family felt fortunate to be still alive."

Azwari drove us through the city. "Would you pray against injustice in Libya?" Azwari asked. "Our prisons are full of foreigners who have been unjustly accused. All a Libyan has to do is accuse a foreigner, and they are imprisoned. For example, if someone doesn't want to pay a foreign worker from India or the Philippines, they just say, 'He takes drugs.' The employer could owe the worker a year's pay, but the worker goes to prison, so the employer does not have to pay. Then they hire another unsuspecting foreigner."

Driving past a university, he told us about how Qaddafi's daughter decided to attend law school. "So, this coed part of the university was forced to become a women-only college for four years. Some young men in their final year of schooling had to travel hundreds of miles to finish school in another city."

"What was the reaction of the students?" Markus asked.

"Well, we live in a country where no one reacts," Azwari told us.

"As a teenager, I couldn't take my exams and finish my grade unless I witnessed an execution." Azwari looked away from us.

"When I was in middle school," Azwari continued, "Five university students spoke out to say there was a better way to do something at their university. For this, one young woman was shot, and the four men were hung. Their parents and family were forced to watch. They pleaded for the lives of the students. It didn't help," a tear formed in the corner of his eye. "I still have nightmares...One boy didn't die right away when they hung him. They pulled on his legs to finish him," Azwari parked the car and rubbed his eyes slowly. "You learn not to react."

"Three years ago, three 19-year-olds were executed for surfing the Internet. But no one can say anything," he said. "School children and others were forced to watch."

We pulled up in front of our hotel.

"Tomorrow night, I want to take you to meet some believers," Azwari said.

I nodded as he put the car into gear and pulled away. The reality of Libya's situation began to weigh on me. What would God want me to share with the people tomorrow?

Before the meeting, we circled the neighborhood to be sure we weren't being followed. That evening, we arrived at a home at the edge of Tripoli where Azwari had gathered seven key people in an upper room. As we walked in, one of the men recognized me.

"Loren! It's you!" he exclaimed. "This brings us so much hope, that you have come."

We began with prayer for Libya. After seeing the capital and hearing Azwari's shocking stories, our team was stirred to pray fervently. "God, would you free these people from the deception and injustice they live under?" Magdy prayed.

Following prayer, the people began to describe Libya to us. Their hearts were burdened by the spiritual darkness and injustice in the nation. "What can we do? If we speak, we will die. If we do not speak, the evil goes on," one man explained with a look of frustration. Then, the man leading the gathering invited me to speak to the group.

I began by telling them of my visit to the mosque in Central Asia, where I'd repented on behalf of the Christian Crusaders. I told them how the angry Muslim cleric had offered me the grapes as a symbol of reconciliation. "Forgiveness and reconciliation remove the barriers to knowing Jesus."

One of the people there spoke up, "I agree. My family spent several weeks in Turkey asking forgiveness for the Crusades. It is imperative."

Our host said, "This is right. I am going to begin asking people to forgive."

I continued by telling the group about a time I flew over the Amazon rainforest. Another passenger, the chairman of the World Wildlife Fund, explained that rainforests have poor soil that's only renewed by the mulch from fallen plants and trees. If a forest's greenery is destroyed, the rains will cease. It would become a desert. The vegetation itself pulls down the moisture and brings life.

"So you see, your presence is like the spiritual greenery that pulls down the blessings of God into the land. You are Libya's source of blessing."

They told me about a Libyan man who was one of their first new believers.

"I am not afraid to die for my Savior Jesus. I only feel bad because they will kill my family when they know I have become a Christian," he told them. The statement rang in my ears as the group waited to hear my response.

I addressed them, saying, "Do you know that the word Christian is only used once in the Bible? It simply says that 'Antioch is where they were first called Christians.' The Bible doesn't tell you to go into all the world and preach about Christianity. What does that word mean? It means one thing to one person and another thing to another. To so many, it has cultural connotations that have nothing to do with the gospel."

Azwari chimed in, "Yes, I am the first Christian my Muslim friends have ever seen in their lives. At Christmas time, they said, 'Oh, we know what you Christians do! You're going to go and get drunk and sleep with several women. That's what Christians do at Christmas.' I told them, 'No, I don't do that because I know Jesus.'"

I smiled and said, "Exactly! When they hear "Christian," they only think of Crusades, bombings, corruption, or immorality. So when you say, 'I'm a Christian', they say, 'Yes, we have heard of you.' But when you talk about Jesus, He is respected as a true prophet, even in the Koran. And prophets only tell the truth. So you can say, 'This is what the teachings of Jesus are. I follow Jesus and his teachings.'"

The leader's eyes widened as it dawned on him.

I continued, "God has given this nation a destiny. And you can begin to fulfill that destiny."

Then, one person got up and said, "I know part of Libya's destiny! It is compassion. After being so badly treated, Libyans have compassion for others who have been badly treated."

I nodded in agreement. In a few minutes, I finished my message, and our group rose to leave. Just before leaving, Azwari explained to the group, "This is Loren's final nation to visit. He has now been a missionary to every country on earth."

One man blurted out, "This is a sign from God." He pointed to the others in the group, "We believe God is saying that very soon the breakthrough is coming."

"I believe you are right!" I answered.

The meeting finished, and we returned to our hotel full of joy. When I finally flew home, I felt new hope and expectation about what God would do in Libya and the Muslim world.

JESUS IS WINNING

In Libya in 1997, I finished my mission to visit every nation and dependent country, but not my life's mission. Until the very end, there is more!

The steps I have taken in missions gained significance because of the many Youth With A Mission workers who counted the cost and answered the call. YWAM teams and many other followers of Jesus have demonstrated God's love in every country. But our mission is far from complete. Every new child born into this world deserves a chance to know what Christ did for them on the cross. They'll only know if we go.

In every corner of the globe, even dark and unreached places like Libya, there are remnants of believers. Some statisticians say there are countries without a single believer in Jesus. Bhutan, the "hermit kingdom" that violently opposed the gospel, was estimated to have 0% of believers in their population in 1985. A remnant was there, but it was hidden. I know of Bhutanese believers and others from every nation on earth.

So, is the world reached? Haven't we finished Jesus' Great Commission if there are believers in every nation? No.

Much remains to be done. We know it because two verses in Revelation say that "every tribe and language and people and nation"[60] will be around the throne of God. What was translated here as "nation" is from the word *ethne*, which would be more accurate if translated as "ethnicity" or "people group." We

---

60. Revelation 7:9

still don't know all the world's tribal groups. God's Word promises that these people groups, with many different mother tongues and customs, will all be reached.

More people are alive now than those who lived from Adam until the beginning of the 20th Century. There will be more than eight billion people on Earth in this decade. Billions of them have never heard the message of Jesus.

The Speed of Darkness

The gospel is spreading far and wide through Asia, Africa, and even the Middle East. I've met with witnesses who reported seeing spiritual revival breaking out in China and Iran. Although we face many difficulties in Asia and the Middle East, the good news of Jesus is being heard. Yet, haven't we been told that things will only turn worse until Jesus comes? Many people don't believe Jesus is or should be winning until the end. There's a school of thought that says believers should be hiding from end-time destruction, not pushing to win, not doing the Great Commission. This fearful view of Biblical prophecy is often portrayed in apocalyptic movies and ominous end-times novels.

Yet this view seems to miss the larger picture. Jesus wins in the end—not the Antichrist. "The earth will be filled with the knowledge of the glory of the LORD.[61]" Though the darkness will deepen, the light of Jesus will spread uncontrollably.

Jesus said, "I am coming soon," so we will stand without fear. Fear is the opposite of faith. A correct understanding of scripture will inspire faith in God, not fear.

God is not afraid of Satan or any antichrist. The book of Revelation tells about how Jesus will be victorious over the enemy. We cannot let this be switched around in our thinking.

---

61. Habakuk 2:14

Believers should question any Bible teaching that paralyzes people with fear or sedates them with apathy.

Revelation does describe disasters, wars, and persecution from the enemy. It also says that the believers will overcome the enemy "by the blood of the Lamb and by the word of their testimony.[62]"

These overcoming believers are fearless men and women who don't "love their lives so much as to shrink from death." They aren't cowering in fear.

These scriptures portray extreme conflict but not doom. They depict two extremes of light and darkness. Each side is increasing. As the Great Commission nears completion, the world is becoming polarized. In the same way that individuals who reject the gospel become jaded, nations can also become hardened to God's love. And just as some individuals respond to God's grace, some countries are seeing multitudes turn to Christ. As the knowledge of God's glory spreads, people must decide—light or darkness?

The knowledge of God brings each person to their day of decision. Many will accept Jesus. Many will reject Him. Few will be left on the fence.

All Will Hear

Scripture clearly says the gospel will be preached to all the world. Some still attack that very idea. A church elder once told William Carey, a pioneer of modern missions, "Young man, sit down. When God pleases to convert the heathen, he will do it without your aid or mine." Today, some justify their inaction by saying, "The world is worse than ever. We just have to hold on till Jesus comes."

Of course, Jesus is coming. That fact must fuel action, not complacency. When Jesus described the end of the world, he

---

62. Revelation 12:11

said, "...this gospel of the kingdom will be preached in the whole world as a testimony to all nations, and then the end will come."

Note the order: First, the gospel of the kingdom will be preached in the whole world. Then the end will come. Our God has unlimited ability to wield supernatural power. He could easily astound, inspire, or even terrify the world into submission. But what God wants most is for people to choose Him like He chose us. The Lord wants people who will choose to love and fulfill His desires.

God chose a closer, more relational way to call every nation to His arms. He decided to send His message through people— people like you and me. The Lord chose to give us this calling, this crucial task of bringing His message to the world.

The earth will be reached by people who shake off complacency. His Word should travel through our lips and our lives. Then, earth's end will finally come after the message of God's love has gone the distance. "Every nation, tribe, people, and language will hear God's message, "and then the end will come.[63]»

Doom and Gloom Deception

One of my greatest joys during my travels has been witnessing the signs of hope worldwide. I've had the privilege to see that Jesus *is* winning. Many news networks do their best to amplify the fears and animosity surrounding global events. Because of this doom and gloom, it is difficult for the public to see what is going on.

Because of YWAM's missionaries scattered across the globe, we often have the privilege of hearing firsthand accounts of international events. The truth can be very different from the reports we see in the media. Once, I was driving with some

63. Matthew 24:14

YWAMers in Egypt near a downtown museum. We felt no danger, but earlier that day, a militant group planted a bomb on a bus outside the museum. It detonated, spraying shrapnel through the bus. Thankfully, the bomb didn't kill anyone or cause significant damage to the museum. Some did have injuries that required medical treatment.

The bombing wasn't much of a story. It was intended to kill and maim people and scare others, but it mostly failed in that objective. More people in Cairo were injured in car accidents during one hour that day than by the bombing. All was peaceful when we drove by the museum. But when I flipped on the news later that night, I saw flames billowing from the bus wreckage and wounded passengers weeping and bleeding in a graphic news report.

Had it happened? Yes. There were no faked video effects in the footage. But the news package that aired portrayed Egypt as a battle zone for extremists. By not showing the bigger picture of this unfazed mega-city, the report manipulated viewers' emotions and broadcast this unbalanced report to a global audience.

The world only saw those moments of terror. Viewers did not realize Egypt was fine and no one had died. This failed act of terrorism became a success through the media's coverage. The report likely scared away tourists and investors, making it a blow to Egypt's economy. This is one story among a multitude. Imagine the combined impact of skewed journalism on the world's economy and society's emotional well-being.

To perceive God's hope for humanity, we must be able to see through distortions and recognize the truth. We must open our eyes to a bigger picture of the world without succumbing to numbness or terror. How can we see the world from a godly perspective?

Imagine if you were watching your favorite sports team on TV. But instead of watching the whole game, the cameras only focus on the opponent's scores. This is what it is like when we read most news reports or watch televised news programs.

"If it bleeds, it leads" has been the slogan of journalism for generations. But this preoccupation with tragedy leaves us staring at the enemy's scores, unable to see our side's victories. It doesn't help to shut off the news. We need to know what the world is seeing and thinking.

We need a fuller picture of what God is doing through His people. A broader perspective is essential for you to live your callings. You cannot see the world transformed until you see it as it is. You cannot live a life of faith if you live in fear.

To be free of fear and numbness, we must learn to read the news from a faith perspective. Only God has a full view of what is happening on earth. But it can be challenging to focus on Him while taking in a constant flow of news media.

One way to keep your focus is to let news drive you to prayer. You shouldn't carry these worries and cares alone. By placing the world into God's hands, you'll be practicing your calling of prayer and making a real difference.

The more you understand of His world, the more effective you will be in pursuing God's purposes. If you overcome fear with faith, God can entrust greater things to you. Everything of lasting benefit is born in faith.

Saturation Evangelism

The more I experience the world, the more I see that Jesus will not just win; He's already winning.

The truth of God is spreading through Asia's underground house churches. His message is being broadcast through Sat 7, the Christian television satellite that transmits across the Middle East. Create International's films share the good news in the local language and culture. Throughout history, there have been great divisions and even wars between Christians. These hindered the growth of the church and pushed many away. Yet so many rifts are being healed through initiatives like the Global Day of Prayer, Call2All, and Calling All Nations. Believers around the world are in a unique season of repentance and unity. This hurting world is poised for the good news of Jesus.

The Word is traveling farther and faster than ever before. The gospel is airborne through our use of modern aviation.

A trip to China took months for pioneer missionary Hudson Taylor. Now, airlines from China make regular flights to and from every continent. What took months now takes hours. The rapid development of the internet and multi-cultural megacities has opened a unique window of time for saturation evangelism.

Most unreached nations on Earth are already online. With a mobile device, you can instantly chat with unreached people— by text, voice, or video. Even a jet ride is slower than a text or online chat. The speed of personal communication to listeners in remote places has gone from months to hours to seconds.

The closed nations that censor the gospel and persecute believers all have first-generation immigrants from their people throughout the Americas and Europe. They are ready to be reached. Tyrants and terrorists drove multitudes of refugees to these cities. But what they meant for evil, God can turn to good.

We are approaching the time God described, saying, "I will pour out My Spirit on all flesh; Your sons and your daughters shall prophesy…And it shall come to pass that whoever calls on the name of the Lord shall be saved.[64]"

Who will ride this tide, propelled by God's Spirit? Who will see the signs of the times and know what must be done?

---

64. Joel 2:28,32 ESV

TRILLION-TO-ONE DESTINY

We often hear about "thinking outside the box." But what if you lived outside the box? Jesus didn't do chamomile parables or predictable healings. He shook things up. The Master broke down boundaries between the establishment and the outcasts—male and female, Jew and Gentile, leper and clean. As he perfectly lived the will of God, no man-made limits could confine him, not even death.

Despite angry crowds and treacherous religious leaders, Jesus was never afraid to walk away from their demands. With His example in mind, consider His ultimate purpose in your life. What were you created for? Are you committed to walk His narrow path? No one can live God's purposes while trapped in human expectations or empty traditions.

The human genome has three billion letters of DNA in a trillion possible combinations that make you, you. If you factor in the risks of car crashes, fatal diseases, crime, or other misfortunes, it is a miracle you even exist.

Given your improbable origin with trillion-to-one odds, there's no doubt God has a special mission for you. Enemies within—like fear, unbelief, and confusion—will hinder you from achieving it. Outside enemies will work to discourage and divert you from the purposes God has for your time here on earth.

Jesus warned us, "You will be hated by everyone because of my name." People will attack you because of mistaken expectations, culturally entrenched misconceptions, or pointless hatred.

If you try to do anything beyond mediocrity, there will be mockers at your side hoping to yank you down to their level.

It is easy to give in as Peter did in denying Christ. It is easy to trade away blessings cheaply—like Esau's birthright sold for a bowl of beans.

The Bible usually gives greater detail about righteous men and women. Multiple books tell the stories of David, Paul, Moses, Samuel, and others. But Judges has six little verses about an entire generation of Israel. The Bible dismisses them as "…another generation grew up who did not acknowledge the LORD or remember the mighty things he had done for Israel."[65]

It is sobering to survey the vast historical record of the Bible and see how many people seem to be clueless sinners who missed the point of life.

The odds are against you. Your environment is hostile. Jesus says, "The road is difficult, and only a few ever find it.[66]"

Many people never live their mission. Their lives are spent appeasing their enemies and living within their walls. Will you waste hours, days, years, or more of your life to please your enemies? Or will you live beyond the world's boundaries in the mission you were made for?

In your mother's womb, God called you. He gave you gifts to complement your call. It is your destiny to answer His call. That is why you were born. You are a gift from God—to all of us and all the world. Don't reject what God has designed to come through your life.

It does not matter how long you've put Him off. It does not matter how dark your life has become. You have a destiny. Don't miss it.

---

65. Judges 2:10 NLT
66. Matthew 7:14 NLT

God wants to purify you to prepare you for His Spirit. When your heart is ready, He will fill you. His Spirit empowers you to accomplish His purposes.

Paul wrote to Timothy, "Take hold of the eternal life to which you were called."[67] Eternal life does not wait for death. Good or bad, each person's eternity has already begun. It is up to you to lay hold of your eternal life calling.

On earth, you are dating your eternity. In death, you will marry that eternity. "For the Son of Man is going to come in his Father's glory with his angels, and then he will reward each person according to what he has done (Matt. 16:27)."

What is your eternity like? Is it passionate and holy, or is it tragic and frightening? Salvation is your first chance to begin living your eternal destiny, the time to start living God's dreams. If you aren't living "the eternal life to which you were called," repent. Change now. Ask God to forgive you and change your heart. Then let God purify you. Let Him fill you with His Spirit and guide you to His purposes.

God has no limits—in prayer, giving, communicating, and going. There are no limits on the gifts and callings God gave you at conception. You begin living those purposes by entering the door of Jesus opened to us through salvation.

That's when God begins sanctification, the lifelong process of purification. Jesus prayed for all believers, asking the Father, "Sanctify them by the truth; your word is truth."[68] Jesus Himself prayed for you to be cleansed. God is ready to wash away all the destructive things He never intended for you.

There is nothing to stop God's designs as you take hold of them in the Spirit. Every boundary, every lie, and every pattern of sin can be broken through the power of Jesus. Anything said or done against you to wreck God's intentions can be defeated.

67. 1 Tim 6:12
68. John 17:17

Jesus died so you could live unafraid and unashamed. His grace can empower you to bold actions worthy of His name. His Spirit will guide you through the details as you listen.

There are no limits to God's dreams for you. You can go anywhere and everywhere, He says. Do anything and everything God calls you to do. You are destined to be "made complete with all the fullness of life and power that comes from God."[69] You're perfectly prepared to respond when the Master says, "Follow me."

---

69. Ephesians 3:19 NLT

MY FINAL CHAPTER

At 88 years old, I am following my calling toward eternity. Walking in His will, aligned to His Word, there is no end to what is possible. It can go on forever.

Our limited perspective only sees challenges, like completing the Great Commission or addressing world hunger.

We try to add it all up. *How many Bibles? How many meals? What do we lack to finish the task?*

In contrast, Revelation 7 describes the paradise to come. People dressed in white around the throne of God. The redeemed nations, tribes, and tongues are all praising Jesus.

Never again will they hunger; never again will they thirst.

It's a multitude "no one can count," every generation from Mother Eve and Father Adam until you.

People ask, Is this the time for Jesus' return?

Yet there's so much more to do!

Seeing the risen Jesus, the apostles asked, "Lord, are you at this time going to restore the kingdom to Israel?"[70]

That's not your business, He explained. That's for the Father to decide. Your job is to be my witnesses to the ends of the earth.

God designed you while you were in your mother's womb. The Bible echoes this. In Psalms 139, He says you are "fearfully and wonderfully made."

---

70. Acts 1:6

You are gifted from before birth like the prophet Isaiah, called from the womb and gifted to speak.[71]

Wrap your heart around your Father's desire to have an immense family. And we're a part of it! We have an elder brother, Jesus, as Romans 8 tells us.[72]

We call God our Father, Abba, Daddy, Papa. As part of the family of God, we're called to rule and reign with Christ forever. So, we must look at things we do here on earth without boundaries.

In 2010, Youth With A Mission was celebrating fifty years of ministry. Darlene and I traveled to meet YWAM staff in 44 locations by taking 107 flights. We had teams in Kona, Hawaii, praying around the clock all year. At the end of that year of intense travel, not even one plane was late for more than two minutes. There were no storms to survive nor terrible turbulence. It was all so smooth and wonderful.

In that remarkable time, 32,000 joined us to sign YWAM's Jubilee Covenant.[73] Some were there beyond our current YWAM staff. Most of our staff couldn't come and sent representatives to one of the 44 locations. What was enormous for us then is still so small in His vast family.

---

71. Isaiah 49:1-2
72. Romans 8:15
73. https://ywam.org/about-us/jubilee-covenant
    I. To love the Lord my God with all my heart, soul, mind and strength, and to love my neighbor as myself (Mark 12:30-21)
    II. To seek first His kingdom and His righteousness above every concern for my own life and future (Matthew 6:25-34)
    III. To serve others for no greater reason than my love for God (John 21:15-17)
    IV. To take up my cross and follow Jesus wherever He leads me (Mark 8:34-35)
    V. To do everything I can possibly do through the power of the Holy Spirit at work in me to fulfill the Great Commission in this generation (Mark 16:15)

MY FINAL CHAPTER   135

The Father doesn't talk about us as numbers. He speaks of "all the world" and "all the nations."[74] The "Alls" and "Everys" of our world still haven't heard. They have never been given the gospel of Jesus, the only way to enter the Father's great family.

Consider the islands of the Pacific. In Pacifica, you can see 1,072 populated islands of Micronesia, Melanesia, and Polynesia. In just one country, Papua New Guinea, they have 291 populated islands and 853 languages.

How do you get God's Word in every language? How do you reach every tribe, every village? The only way to do this is to multiply. The ones you reach and teach are your multiplication. They will touch more hearts than you ever could alone. All nations, tribes, peoples, and tongues: that is what our goal should be. No boundaries.

In Pacifica, you have over 10,000 islands with millions living on them. So many are isolated, with no airstrips or ports.

A thousand kilometers south of Japan's main islands, I sailed to the archipelago of Ogasawara Islands. There were no flights to get there, only the long sea voyage. They have more than two thousand people on two islands, but just one Lutheran church, started generations ago by German missionaries.

Tristan da Cunha is easily one of the most isolated places on earth. To get there, one must go to the southern tip of Africa and then west for one week on a mail boat—the one and only boat per year. I was on it. With an invitation from a local pastor, they let me set foot ashore and speak at his church. They only had two, one Anglican and one Catholic, for 455 people. No airstrips. No TV, no regular connection to the outside world.

In 2008, Darlene and I visited twelve locations and four workstations in Antarctica. Alv Magnus flew with me to the Arctic isles of Svalbard, three hours by jet north of Tromsø, the

---

74. Matthew 24:14, 28:19

northernmost major airport in Norway. We landed on ice in a place with only 2,000 people.

These are the ends of the earth we cannot forget. Each one matters to the Father. They await footprints from faithful, fearless sons and daughters.

My Long Journey Home

On November 17, 2022, I knew something was terribly wrong. Sharp pains began to jolt my chest. The pain amped up, shooting through my upper body without warning. In time, it hurt too much to touch many parts of my body. Just moving in bed would trigger severe pain.

At the hospital in Hawaii, the doctors determined there was a blood infection. *But was that it?* Word of this went out, and YWAM friends began praying worldwide. One intercessor prayed for me and saw something dark in my chest.

Tests began. Initial scans showed small nodules in my lungs, too small to test. By December, they had grown large enough for doctors to do a lung biopsy. Test results showed it was cancerous.

In January, two doctors confirmed that chemo and treatment were not viable. Early on, I received a verse that confirmed it, "Elisha had fallen sick with the illness of which he was to die."[75]

In Honolulu, they administered a full-body PET scan on February 22nd. It revealed extensive cancer in my lungs, bones, and lymph system.

Stage 4 small-cell lung cancer is rapid in most cases. The oncologist said, "Usually, lesions in the lungs grow quickly. Loren's have grown slowly and haven't presented in the brain."

"What is your pain level?" the doctor asked.

"Zero!" I said.

---

75. 2 Kings 13:14-20 ESV

"That's impossible!" the doctor said. "That's so unusual."

Dar responded, "Well, this man has always been unusual! And we have a great God and many people praying for him!"

From December 2022 through August 2023, the prayers increased, and the debilitating pain disappeared. But further tests confirmed the cancer was spreading. Yet somehow, I could speak online daily with thousands of youth, staff, and leaders from our home in Kona.

At our big meeting pavilion in Kona, I spoke with our staff in July. "The doctors only gave me weeks, but it's been eight months!" I chuckled. The people cheered as they heard what God had done. But some worried looks remained.

After one of the talks, Dar wrote to update friends and family, "He looks so good. No one would guess what we are facing!"

For me, my family, and mission friends, there's no wonder why this is all happening. My time is being extended for the greatest purpose God's ever entrusted to me—a vision that took me back to my childhood.

From the Moon to the Multitudes

Young men see visions. Old men dream dreams. As I battle cancer, my heart is stirred by a recurring dream, a multitude in heaven. The most significant vision I can imagine is to get the Bible and the message of Jesus into every language on earth.

As a small boy, I wanted to reach everybody in the world with God's Word. I thought, *Well, I know what I'll do. I'll get to the moon.*" Nobody had gone yet.

"I'll put big rocks to spell out 'for God so loved the world that He gave us His only son," from John 3:16.

Then I realized, "No, I can't work with that many rocks." So I ended up with "God is love."[76] That was my child-like dream.

---

76. 1 John 4:8 NASB

We say in the Lord's Prayer, "Your kingdom come. Your will be done. On earth as it is in heaven."[77]

So, what is being done in heaven that's not on earth?

Is it solving world hunger? No, the "daily bread" we pray for on earth is abundant in heaven. Hunger, temptation, and sin will all pass away.

What's missing is worship. There in Revelation 5, they are worshiping the Lamb, Jesus. In Chapter 7, the redeemed are robed in white, worshiping in a multitude no one can count.

In heaven, all mother tongues will be raised to honor the King. The languages of heaven will never cease their worship. This is what we pray to be done on earth as it is in heaven.

On earth, there are thousands of languages, and most of these mother tongues still don't have the Bible or can use their language to worship "in Spirit and in truth."[78]

Why do mother tongues matter so much? A loving mother's voice gives nurture, trust, and care that shapes us before birth. Scientific study shows that babies begin to recognize speech patterns and emotions by the second trimester of pregnancy.[79]

At Pentecost, when the Holy Spirit came in a violent wind, "they were all filled with the Holy Spirit and began to speak with different tongues, as the Spirit was giving them the ability to speak out."[80]

They did not speak in Jerusalem's trade languages like Aramaic, Greek, or Hebrew. As fire rested on them, they were given the heart languages of "Parthians, Medes, and Elamites, and residents of Mesopotamia, Judea, and Cappadocia, Pontus

77. Matthew 6:10 NKJV
78. John 4:23 NASB
79. Prenatal auditory experience and its sequelae - Marin Vogelsang, Lukas Vogelsang, Sidney Diamond, Pawan Sinha - Developmental Science - Volume 26, Issue 1, January 2023
80. Acts 2:4 NASB

and Asia, Phrygia and Pamphylia, Egypt, and parts of Libya around Cyrene…Cretans and Arabs.

In mother tongues, they spoke of the mighty deeds of God. That day, three thousand were saved and baptized. This is the origin story of God's "kingdom come on earth as it is in heaven." In it, I see the same fire that will ignite revival in this generation and across the globe.

Some 200 million people still speak a mother tongue without a single verse of Scripture. They have never heard God's Word in their trusted heart language.

In Zephaniah, it says, "Then I will purify the speech of all people, so that everyone can worship the LORD together."[81] He is looking forward, showing us His dream of every tongue celebrating together in the throne room of heaven. His goal is for all mother tongues, everywhere on earth.

YWAM teams on the ground are already working to map out remote and diverse regions in Nigeria, Papua New Guinea, Nepal, and Mexico to get God's Word into their heart languages. Word came from mapping teams in Mexico recently that 50 more mother tongues without Scripture have been located!

At 88 years old, as I fight cancer, God is giving me visions of how to get God's Word to every people group, tribe, and mother tongue.

How can they all hear and believe?

Why not record an oral Bible in the mother tongue of every people group on earth?

As my time draws near, I am convinced that this is how the world will hear and trust God's Word.

Their oral mother tongue, or "OMT" translations of Scripture, can stir the hearts of ethnic communities.

81. Zephaniah 3:9 NLT

Young visionaries like you can pray and journey with a team to the diverse linguistic regions of the world—Latin America, Africa, Pacifica, Asia, or native tribes and subcultures.

Go deeper than I have gone—beyond nations and territories—to find mother tongue languages that need Scripture. Then, find three or more native speakers who will help get the Bible presented in their mother tongue. Find the ones who also speak a trade language with Scripture, like English, Spanish, French or Mandarin. These mother tongue speakers are adept in their expressions, vocabulary, and culture. They can translate scripture from a trade language into their own mother tongue—checking it with the team of three and their community.

When mapping is done in an area, you could help with recording, serve mother tongue translators, and share OMT recordings with eager locals.

The OMT recordings fit on memory cards the size of my fingernail and work in the simplest mobile phones. YWAM volunteers trekking on rugged trails have found phones like this even in remote Himalayan villages. The villagers used solar charges to enable these mobile devices. Since they have no internet, someone travels to larger cities to get music to share in the village.

Why not give the people a Bible to hear in their mother tongue? It would fulfill my 1956 vision of waves of youth from everywhere to everywhere. Imagine missionaries from every mother tongue joining the Great Commission!

For five centuries, we relied on print. Now, with digital recording and distribution, the oral storytelling cultures of native peoples can be strengthened. You can honor and empower mother tongue speakers to speed the translation of God's Word.

All of this can begin once you pray and set out to find them. As you find these unreached people and locations, record their GPS coordinates and connect them with our PrayOMT.com site.

Jeremy, a young YWAMer, messaged me during his team's outreach to a Nepali people group near the border of India. "For 13 years, they have been working on vocabulary, hoping to get a Bible into their language. Now they want to finish in one year!" Fifteen pastors from that region are "all in" for joining the OMT vision.

Like the man who found the Mossis, God can lead you to the ends of the earth. And just like the Mossis, their tribes and cultures will find redemption and reformation.

There are not smooth roads to every tribe and tongue. You must go offroad into cultures you've never dreamed of meeting. You will experience places far different than you've ever known. This year, a team in Madang, Papua New Guinea, found a tribe that had never known of an outside world until eight years ago. That is truly the "ends of the earth."

It's the kind of challenge I got in my youth—to go into all the world for the gospel's sake.

In our early schools in Europe between 1969 and 1970, we laid maps on the floor. Young students prayed over the maps. *Where will we go?*

One by one, they prayed and got a nation. In just five years, they were out there serving. Teams went across Africa and others to India, Nepal, and Afghanistan, all because they prayed and God said, "Go." God spoke to them as He speaks to you.

Now, we can pray and go deeper than geography. Go to the depths of what shapes each person's culture and identity. Go to all mother tongues.

There are one billion adults who cannot read, one out of every seven people on earth. How will these masses receive God's Word in a way they can respond to?

The Bible says in the beginning, "God spoke." It didn't say He wrote. Man wrote it down, but God spoke. And God still speaks.

God says, "faith comes by hearing, and hearing by the word of God."[82] He speaks orally.

Jesus said, "My sheep hear My voice, and I know them, and they follow Me."[83]

So you can hear and follow Him as far as He may lead—beyond borders and boundaries.

Find your Mossis—the mother tongue group God's guiding you to. Pray. Serve. Honor.

As you find your mother tongue people and their experts to translate God's Word, Bible translation can begin. Join our OMT efforts at PrayOMT.com

This final dream of mine can be yours. As I prepare for the end, I don't hope to "pass my torch" on to another. I pray I might light the torches of many who will continue until His Kingdom comes. Many can take hold of this, the most incredible vision I could ever imagine. The multitude in Heaven will swell in eternity because bold hearts on earth follow God now to record Scripture in every mother tongue.

When you hear the news that I have gone on to heaven, I hope you remember this call and respond.

---

82. Romans 10:17 NKJV
83. John 10:27 NASB